It's About Time

The Competitive Advantage of
Quick Response Manufacturing

It's About Time

The Competitive Advantage of Quick Response Manufacturing

RAJAN SURI

CRC Press
Taylor & Francis Group
Boca Raton   London   New York

CRC Press is an imprint of the
Taylor & Francis Group, an **informa** business

A PRODUCTIVITY PRESS BOOK

Productivity Press
Taylor & Francis Group
270 Madison Avenue
New York, NY 10016

© 2010 by Taylor and Francis Group, LLC
Productivity Press is an imprint of Taylor & Francis Group, an Informa business

No claim to original U.S. Government works

Printed in the United States of America on acid-free paper
10 9 8 7 6 5 4 3

International Standard Book Number: 978-1-4398-0595-4 (Hardback)

Library of Congress Cataloging-in-Publication Data

Suri, Rajan.
    It's about time : the competitive advantage of quick response manufacturing / Rajan Suri.
        p. cm.
    Includes index.
    ISBN 978-1-4398-0595-4 (hard back : alk. paper)
    1. Production management. 2. Production scheduling. 3. Manufacturing cells. 4. New products. I. Title.

TS155.S888 2010
658.5--dc22   2009052040

Visit the Taylor & Francis Web site at
http://www.taylorandfrancis.com

and the Productivity Press Web site at
http://www.productivitypress.com

To Nicole

Contents

Contents of Bonus CD

The following Appendices are on the enclosed CD. You can also access these Appendices at www.qrmcenter.org.

Acknowledgments

A large number of individuals and organizations have contributed to the theory and practice of Quick Response Manufacturing. Many people who supported my early work and encouraged the development of my ideas were acknowledged in my 1998 book on QRM. Here I acknowledge those who have contributed to furthering the theory and implementation of QRM since the publication of that book.

I would like to begin by thanking Ananth Krishnamurthy who has had both the courage and the conviction to take over the leadership of the Center for Quick Response Manufacturing in 2008, which has given me the opportunity to spend more time doing what I really enjoy most—teaching QRM workshops, writing about QRM, and helping companies implement it. In Ananth's first two years of leadership, the Center has not only stayed the course in spite of difficult economic times, but it has also launched initiatives that should take QRM theory to new levels and QRM practice in new directions. Ananth also provided invaluable comments and advice on the manuscript for this book.

The QRM approach relies heavily on the Manufacturing Critical-path Time (MCT) metric. During his tenure as a supply management professional at two large equipment manufacturers, Paul Ericksen pioneered the development and application of MCT, and partnered with the Center for QRM and professionals at several other companies to prove out the power of MCT. Significant contributions to MCT development were made by Aaron Armstrong, Bashar Eljawhari, Mike Ketter, Sean Ketter, and Nathan Stoflet. Ananth, Mike, and Nathan also helped me refine the MCT example in Appendix A (on the enclosed CD).

Several people provided valuable feedback on my preliminary manuscript, and many, many people have contributed to the development and application of QRM since the publication of my first book. In alphabetical order (by last name) I would like to thank all of these people: Steve Addison, Paul Allen, Jerry Ammann, Jeff Amundson, Hope Anderson, Jennifer Anderson, Jason Bachman, Anirban Banerjee, Avishek Basu, Brian Basler, Tom Becker, Lynn Benishek, Shyam Bhaskar, Hardik Bheda, Alex Bohl, Mike Borden, Alex Bredemus, Bob Briggs, Kyle Brown, Cynthia Bruns, Bill Butterfield, Todd Carlson, Jan Carwardine, Vinay Chauhan, Bob

Charron, Kristi Charron, Jeff Cypher, Mark Dawson, Suzanne de Treville, Bob Dempsey, Jon Denzin, Paul Diedrick, Kari Doyle, Shawn Duffy, Greg Diehl, Al Drifka, Scott Fredrick, Axel Frick, Matthew Friedlander, Kevin Fons, Chuck Gates, Vrushali Gaud, Hans Gerrese, Scott Gilson, Mary Graves, Marty Grell, Steve Griffin, Tracy Gundert, Okan Gurbuz, Tim Hallock, Xiaoyin Han, Todd Hansel, Carly Hanson, Terry Hanstedt, Rob Herman, Laura Holden, Chris Holm, Dave Holmgren, Mark Irwin, Ankur Jain, Neal Johnson, Steve Jorud, Fried Kaanen, Rudi Kerkhofs, Sue Klingaman, Joe Koenig, Jeff Konkel, Mike Koplin, K'uang Ku, Jim Landherr, Genny LeBrun, John Loeffelholz, Gary Lofquist, Warren Long, Harry Loos, Peter Luh, Thomas Luiten, Mary Maedke, Paul Martens, Neil Massey, Ella Mae Matsumura, Dave McKnight, Jitesh Mehta, Jama Meyer, Ryan Mijal, Audrey Miller, Brian Mitchard, Bill Molek, Bob Mueller, Hanns-Peter Nagel, Lori Neils, Terry Nelson, Tom Nelson, Jessica Nguyen, Pat Nienhaus, Mark Oriatti, Patrick Parks, Kathy Pelto, Ron Peterson, Sandy Petranek, Mick Petzold, Frank Piller, Ben Quirt, Frank Rath, Greg Renfro, Pattie Reynolds, Bill Ritchie, Chris Roepe, Mike Root, Debjit Roy, Chaitanya Saha, Sushanta Sahu, Ragini Saxena, Tom Schabel, Tom Schlough, Chris Schluter, Stuart Schmidt, Jeremy Schwartz, Divya Seethapathy, Bill Shager, Shakeel Shaikh, Toby Shaw, Masami Shimizu, Rahul Shinde, Mark Singer, Abhishek Sinkar, Randy Smith, Brian Sobczak, Alex Stoltz, Jim Tennessen, Jan ter Bogt, Roberto Teti, Ron Tews, Manoj Tiwari, Carl Treankler, Atul Tripathi, Jim Truog, Francisco Tubino, Paul van Veen, Nico Vandaele, Raj Veeramani, Rob Voesenek, Kathy Watson, Urban Wemmerlöv, Rosalyna Wijaya, Sara Woitte, Mike Wolfe, Tatsuhiko Yamamoto, and Charlene Yauch.

Over 200 organizations have supported the work of the QRM Center and I am grateful to all of them for their help and encouragement over the years. A complete list of these companies can be found at www.qrmcenter.org

I would also like to thank Maura May and Michael Sinocchi of Productivity Press for supporting the development of this book and Lara Zoble, Tere Stouffer, and Iris Fahrer for their expert help with organizing and editing the manuscript.

Introduction

It has been just over 10 years since Productivity Press published my book *Quick Response Manufacturing: A Companywide Approach to Reducing Lead Times,* which was the first comprehensive publication of the basic principles of Quick Response Manufacturing (QRM), along with techniques and tools for the application of this strategy. At the time the book was published, many of my QRM principles were considered revolutionary as they challenged numerous existing manufacturing management beliefs. During the last 10 years, however, these QRM principles and techniques have been successfully applied at hundreds of companies. Many of these companies have achieved amazing results and their stories have been showcased at conferences around the world, including nine international conferences held at the Center for Quick Response Manufacturing at the University of Wisconsin in Madison. Companies that have adopted QRM—and their employees—display a tremendous enthusiasm for the concept and what it has accomplished for them.

However, I have been told on numerous occasions by "fans" of my first book that even though they enjoyed reading all the details in the 540 pages there, they would like to have a shorter book that they can give to their managers to read—a concise description of QRM that would convince a senior executive to pursue the QRM strategy (540 pages is a bit daunting for a busy executive!). My first goal in writing this book was to address this need. Specifically, this book is intended for busy executives, as something you can get through during a couple of airplane trips or a long weekend. With top management in mind, I adopt a more strategic view of QRM throughout the book with fewer technical details. However, I do cover the core principles of QRM so that executives can understand enough about QRM to support their managers and employees tasked with implementing the details of this strategy. I also use many new explanation approaches along with examples that should appeal to senior management. Having taught QRM workshops for senior executives for over 10 years, I now have a better idea of how to get their attention and what to include for this audience.

A second goal for this book was to have a text that could be read by managers and employees from all functional areas of the company. There were a couple of reasons for this goal. For one, QRM is not just a shop floor technique—as you will see in this book—it is an enterprise-wide strategy. But a more important reason is this: A decade of work with hundreds of companies has shown that for maximum impact of QRM in an organization, people from all functions need to be educated in QRM so that they buy into and support the company-wide implementation. In addition to the obvious target of employees in functions such as manufacturing, materials, and continuous improvement, the audience for this book includes managers and employees in marketing and sales, accounting, human resources, purchasing and supply chain, engineering and R&D, general administration, and IT. It is clear from the evidence that the most successful QRM companies have been the ones that have ensured that everyone in the company, from shop floor workers to senior executives, from clerical staff to chief engineers, has been trained in the core principles of QRM. It is my hope that this book will also serve this broad audience.

Even if you are already familiar with QRM and read the first book, you will still find a lot of value in this book. The decade of experience has helped me to present the core principles of QRM in a new way; the fundamental principles remain unchanged but I use a novel framework for explaining them, and many examples and diagrams are also new. I hope you will appreciate and even enjoy these novelties. In addition, through the partnership of my colleagues at the Center for Quick Response Manufacturing and the managers and employees of all the companies who have worked with the center, several new tools and concepts have been developed to further the theory of QRM and sharpen its application. You will find that this book also contains many new developments beyond the first book.

My final goal for this book was to convince companies of the need for new and bold strategic thinking. With the growth of global competition, with the changes brought about by outsourcing of both manufacturing and support jobs to low-wage countries, and with the difficult economic conditions around the world, companies need to reexamine their competitive strategy. Over the past two decades most manufacturing organizations have looked into or implemented strategies such as Kaizen, Six Sigma, and Lean Manufacturing. However, modern technology is fundamentally changing the variety of products that can be offered to customers as well as the way customers can interact with companies through the Internet, and both these effects are creating new and different levels of customer expectations. You need a strategy that will explicitly take advantage of the market shift that is occurring as a result. In addition, if everyone in your industry is implementing the same strategies of Six Sigma and Lean, what is your competitive edge? It is my goal to convince you the answer is QRM!

In this book, you will learn the **four core concepts** that comprise QRM strategy:

The power of time: While everyone knows that lead time matters, you will learn about the nonobvious reasons why lead time is important (much more important than most managers realize), how it influences total operating cost and quality, and how to take advantage of this realization to change the way that you think about and manage your business. See Chapter 1 of this book.

Organization structure: You will learn how to restructure your organization to minimize lead time throughout the enterprise. A key building block here is the "QRM Cell." Although the cell concept has been in use for several decades, QRM Cells extend this in several ways to achieve new levels of flexibility and team performance. See Chapter 2.

System dynamics: You will gain insight into how interactions between machines, people, and products impact your lead times. As a result, you will rethink your capacity planning approaches (e.g., machine and labor utilization), batch-sizing policies, and other related decisions, to realize systemwide benefits from the new approaches. See Chapter 3.

Enterprise-wide application: QRM is not just a shop floor approach; it is applied throughout the organization. This includes material planning, purchasing and supply chain management, office operations such as estimating and order processing, engineering, and new-product development. You will see how QRM methods extend to your whole enterprise. See Chapter 4.

Of course there is a large gap between understanding a strategy and successfully implementing it. So I conclude the book by giving you a tried-and-tested road map for implementing QRM. Over the past 10 years, I have been involved in hundreds of QRM projects, and this road map is based on the common elements that led to the greatest successes. See Chapter 5.

There are a number of practical details that can assist in the success of your QRM implementation. You do not need to read through these details during your first introduction to QRM strategy, but will want access to them for yourself or your staff as you embark on your QRM efforts. Thus, in keeping with my goals of providing you with a short text that covers the key points of QRM, I have put these details in five Appendices that are on the accompanying CD. (You can also access these Appendices at www.qrmcenter.org) I chose the topics for the Appendices based on numerous experiences with companies, picking those that most frequently needed to be addressed during the implementation. When you are ready to start implementing QRM, you will find that these Appendices contain many tips and pointers that help you work through implementation questions, and they also provide simple calculation methods and tools to support the design of your QRM strategy.

The good news is that you do *not* need to turn your back on any improvement strategies you have already implemented and start over with QRM. Rather, QRM builds on the foundation created by these other methods, but at the same time it takes your competitiveness to the next level needed to be successful in this market. If you can understand and implement QRM before your competition figures out how to do it, huge market opportunities, improved profitability, and a highly stimulating work environment await your enterprise and your employees.

1

The Power of Time

Everyone knows that time is money, *but time is actually a lot more money than most managers realize*! Chuck Gates, president of RenewAire, came to this realization and, using the Quick Response Manufacturing (QRM) methods in this book, he reduced his product lead times by over 80%. As a result, RenewAire, a Madison, Wisconsin–based manufacturer of customized energy recovery ventilation systems, gobbled up market share; this tiny company competing with industry giants multiplied its revenue by 2.4 from 2003 to 2008. At the same time, the company significantly improved its productivity, requiring only a 73% growth in total employees for this big increase in sales. As expected from these numbers, profits also grew accordingly. During these five years, RenewAire increased its market share by 42%—in other words, Chuck is eating his competition's lunch!

At the other end of the spectrum from RenewAire, which makes small systems in a facility with fewer than 100 people, is National Oilwell Varco (NOV), headquartered in Houston, Texas, a company that makes huge equipment used in both offshore and land-based oil drilling and has annual sales of around $10 billion. Managers at one of NOV's factories in Orange, California, also saw the vast impact of time on their operation, and in their very first application of QRM methods, reduced the lead time of one of their customized products from 75 days to 4 days. But that was only the beginning—when the results were evaluated, management at NOV-Orange realized that the cost of that product had also been slashed by over 30%! The results of this first project were so impressive that NOV-Orange expanded the application of QRM to all its products, and now NOV is implementing these QRM techniques in dozens of factories worldwide.

Let me pause to reexamine the 30% cost reduction. This number is significant for two reasons. First, it demonstrates the huge impact that time reduction can have on your whole operation, affecting not only lead time

1

to customers, but also cost, quality, and other measures of operational effectiveness. Second, this 30% number counters a growing concern for companies in the United States and other developed countries. Today, most manufacturing companies and their employees in developed countries live in fear that their operation and their jobs will be outsourced to countries with low labor costs—countries such as China and many others in South Asia, Eastern Europe, and Latin America. But the fact is, for a typical product made in the United States, direct labor accounts for only 10% of its cost (the "cost of goods sold" in accounting terms)—and this number is similar for most developed countries. Moreover, as a percentage of the selling price of a product, the number is much lower: only 5% to 7% of the final price to the customer is attributable to direct labor. Thus, if you can use QRM methods to reduce your cost by 30%—and many companies have achieved or exceeded this number—then you have effectively wiped out the labor-cost advantage of all those other countries. Add to this that domestic production eliminates the costs of shipping from overseas, plus your short response times, and it is impossible for overseas manufacturers to compete on the same terms. You can compete against any manufacturer, making products anywhere!

DEFINING QRM

Quick Response Manufacturing is a company-wide strategy for reducing lead times throughout the enterprise. QRM pursues the reduction of lead time in all aspects of a company's operations, both internally and externally. Specifically, from a customer's point of view, QRM means responding to that customer's needs by rapidly designing and manufacturing products customized to those needs. This is the external aspect of QRM. Next, in terms of a company's own operations, QRM focuses on reducing the lead times for all tasks within the whole enterprise. This is the internal aspect of QRM. Examples of such internal lead times are the time to approve and implement an engineering change or the time to issue a purchase order to a supplier. Typically such lead times are not directly observed by the customer. However, you will see that the application of QRM to reduce these internal lead times results in improved quality, lower cost, and of course, quicker response for the customer.

As I explain in the Introduction, QRM strategy is based on four core concepts: (1) the power of time, (2) organization structure, (3) system dynamics, and (4) enterprise-wide application. The fourth principle—the fact that QRM is not just a shop floor approach—has been a key element in its success. An illustration of just how powerful QRM can be beyond the shop floor is provided by TCI, LLC, a manufacturer of customized power inverters in Milwaukee, Wisconsin. When TCI received an order for a customized inverter, it used to take the company over a week in office operations before the order was released to the shop floor. By applying QRM methods, TCI was able to reduce this time from over a week to just one hour!

But what if you have already invested in other strategies such as Total Quality, Six Sigma, or Kaizen? Adopting QRM does not require you to back away from any of these. On the contrary, you will see in this book that QRM helps to complement and build on these strategies and at the same time unify them under one overarching goal—reducing lead time.

And what if you have embarked on a major program to implement Lean Manufacturing? Again, QRM will enhance your Lean program and take it to the next level. To see this, consider that the origins of Lean are in the Toyota Production System, with high-volume, repetitive production. Thus the strategy on which Lean is based was designed for situations with relatively stable demand and largely for replacement products with high volume. However, in the past several years there has been rapid growth in the number of options provided by manufacturers to their customers. Even beyond providing prespecified options, though, is the fact that today's CAD/CAM technology has given companies the ability to custom-engineer and then manufacture products for individual clients without incurring the high additional costs that such customization would have required two decades ago. Along with this has come the power of the Internet, which allows customers to easily view many different options and select from them, with some Web sites even giving customers the ability to specify additional features that may require engineering. All of these developments mean that in the twenty-first century there will be increasing demand for low-volume, high-variety products with options configured for individual customers or even custom-engineered for each client. I will use the term "twenty-first century markets" to refer to this type of growing demand in the twenty-first century.

How does this all relate to Lean? The core techniques in Lean, such as takt times and kanban, are designed to eliminate variability in operations so as to create "flow" (also a Lean concept). This works well for higher volumes and replacement products, but may not be the right strategy for low-volume, high-variety, or customized products. An insight into variability helps to sharpen this point and to clarify how QRM can enhance your Lean program. I define two types of variability. The first I call *dysfunctional variability*, which is caused by errors, ineffective systems, and poor organization. Examples of dysfunctional variability are: rework, constantly changing priorities and due dates, and "lumpy" demand due to poor interfaces between sales and customers. The second type of variability I call *strategic variability*, which an organization uses to maintain its competitive edge in the market. Examples of strategic variability are: the ability to cope with unexpected changes in demand without degradation of service, offering a large number of options to customers, and offering custom-engineered products for individual applications.

The core Lean techniques aim to eliminate all variability in the manufacturing system. This is good as far as eliminating dysfunctional variability is concerned. However, you may not want to eliminate strategic variability, particularly if it is the basis of your competitive advantage. The QRM approach is aligned with the Lean approach in trying to get rid of all dysfunctional variability. However, in QRM you do not eliminate strategic variability, instead you exploit it! This is done by designing the QRM organization and support systems to effectively cope with this variability and serve those customer markets well. These markets are, in fact, the twenty-first century markets just described. Hence, QRM takes the Lean strategy to the next level, appropriate for the twenty-first century (see Figure 1.1).

CHALLENGES TO REDUCING LEAD TIME

Most managers understand the competitive advantages of being fast in responding to customers, and companies are attempting to improve their responsiveness. However, there are many misconceptions about how to reduce lead times and implement quick response. These misconceptions prevent successful results. My early experiences in implementing QRM led me to develop a simple quiz, which I have used to document the state of manufacturing management strategy. Before I present the results, you may find it interesting to take the QRM quiz in Figure 1.2. If you are in

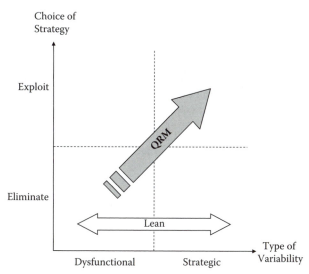

FIGURE 1.1
QRM strategy enhances lean programs.

industry, complete the quiz as follows. For each of the assertions in the quiz, ask yourself: Do the key managers in my company consider this statement to be true or false? If you are in a consulting organization or in academia, choose a company you know that is struggling with lead time reduction, and ask: Do the key managers in that company consider this statement to be true or false? Let me set some ground rules though, to make sure you are being completely ruthless in your evaluation. You need to answer the quiz based on the policies in use at the company, not based on your own opinion of what is correct. Take the first statement in the quiz as an example: Everyone will have to work faster, harder, and longer hours, in order to get jobs done in less time.

As you look at this, you surely think, "We all know that to be false. We need to work smarter, not harder." But then, ask yourself, "Does the company frequently use overtime? Does it take a lot of expediting to get jobs out on time? Do people at the company often have to work on weekends to deal with late jobs?" If the answer to any of these is yes, then it is clear that key managers in the company believe item #1 is true! Use this same probing mind-set as you approach each of the remaining items.

Mark your answers in the boxes in Figure 1.2, and then read on to evaluate the results.

Quiz on Implementing QRM

Developed by Rajan Suri

For each statement below, ask yourself: Would the key managers
in my company consider this statement to be True or False?
Mark your responses in the boxes, then compare them
with the answers given in the text.

1. Everyone will have to work faster, harder, and longer hours, in order to get
   jobs done in less time.
   ❑ True   ❑ False

2. To get jobs out fast, we must keep our machines and people busy all the time.
   ❑ True   ❑ False

3. In order to reduce our lead times, we have to improve our efficiencies.
   ❑ True   ❑ False

4. We must place great importance on "on-time" delivery performance by each
   of our departments, and by our suppliers.
   ❑ True   ❑ False

5. Installing a Material Requirements Planning (MRP or ERP) System will help
   in reducing lead times.
   ❑ True   ❑ False

6. Since long lead time items need to be ordered in large quantities, we should
   negotiate quantity discounts with our suppliers.
   ❑ True   ❑ False

7. We should encourage our customers to buy our products in large quantities
   by offering price breaks and quantity discounts.
   ❑ True   ❑ False

8. We can implement QRM by forming teams in each department.
   ❑ True   ❑ False

9. The reason for implementing QRM is so that we can charge our customers
   more for rush jobs.
   ❑ True   ❑ False

10. Implementing QRM will require large investments in technology.
    ❑ True   ❑ False

Copyright © 1997, 2010 R. Suri.

FIGURE 1.2
Quiz on implementing QRM.

Now I present the answers. Experience with hundreds of QRM projects has shown the following: for successful implementation of QRM it is necessary for a company's key decision makers to believe that every single one of those assertions in the quiz is false! This may be obvious to you in some cases, such as item #1, where you know you have to find ways to work smarter. But what could be wrong with improving efficiencies (item #3)? And isn't on-time delivery (item #4) a cornerstone of every just-in-time (JIT) program? And what about teams (item #8)? Aren't they all the rage these days, in everything from shop floor work to office operations? How could all those assertions possibly be false?

It is precisely these surprising points that I will explain in this book. But what is the significance of these quiz questions and why should they matter to you? Each item for which you answered "true" will, sooner or later, become an obstacle to the success of your QRM program—or worse yet, belief in one of these assertions by a senior manager could increase your lead times instead of reducing them! And, as your lead times get longer, the same senior manager will push harder on that belief, thinking it is not being followed sufficiently, resulting in a vicious cycle of even longer lead times.

To illustrate the magnitude of misconceptions that exist in management circles, I present a simple statistic. I interviewed over 400 U.S. executives and managers in dozens of industries, and even though all of them were from firms that were trying to cut their lead times, 70% of the policies in use by these managers and their companies were major obstacles to lead time reduction. Worse yet, it was not as if these managers were working on changing the policies. In most cases they had no awareness that these policies were the source of the problem. If over two-thirds of the policies in use at an average U.S. firm are preventing it from cutting its lead times, what's the chance that your company also suffers from this malady?

Let us return to your own experience with the quiz. How well did your chosen firm score? Give your company a score of 0 for each true answer and 1 for each false answer. Count up the number of times you checked the false box, and that is your company's score. This score is on a scale of 0 to 10, where 0 denotes a company that will have to undergo a gargantuan change to succeed at QRM, while 10 denotes a company that is a "veteran" of QRM.

In reality, most companies will score somewhere in between. Do not be surprised if your company's score is low. The typical score for a U.S. company is around 3. Interestingly, this average remains true across industry segments, from equipment manufacturers to parts suppliers, and from electronics assembly firms to plastic injection molders. The score also seems to be independent of company size, with firms ranging in size from 50 employees to several thousand scoring in a similar range. Seven out of the ten questions are typically answered "true," which leads to my earlier assertion that 70% of the policies in use at U.S. companies are working against lead time reduction.

The peril of this situation is that not only are the wrong principles in operation, but managers may not know that these principles are wrong. More important than the correct response to each quiz item, however, is an in-depth understanding of why it is the correct response, as well as the numerous issues that must be addressed to change from the current way of operation to the QRM way. Only when management clearly understands the basis for each QRM principle can it lead the organization along the QRM journey. In this book I will explain the key QRM principles and also give you a road map for successful implementation.

QRM FOCUS IS DIFFERENT FROM A TRADITIONAL APPROACH

Each of the items in the QRM quiz illustrates a traditional management belief. We will see that the QRM approach is quite different. I begin by discussing the first item in the quiz, and then provide the QRM principle that must replace it.

- **Traditional Belief #1:** Everyone will have to work faster, harder, and longer hours, in order to get jobs done in less time. This belief is typical of the old way of improving manufacturing—teams of industrial engineers armed with stopwatches performing efficiency studies. Here's a simple reason this won't achieve your goal. You might get a 5% or even 10% increase in speed by giving people better incentives (or threats). But there is a limit to how much you can push a person or a machine—pushed beyond a certain speed, people will be unable to perform tasks reliably, quality will deteriorate, tooling will break down on machines, and so on. In any case, you are certainly not going to achieve the 70% to 80% reductions in lead time that we are aiming for.

- **QRM Principle #1:** Find whole new ways of completing a job, with a primary focus on minimizing lead time. At first glance, it may not be clear that this principle is a departure from traditional manufacturing but it does, in fact, imply a huge shift in mind-set from traditional cost-based thinking to what I will call *time-based thinking*. A simple example helps to drive this home. Figure 1.3 shows the progress of an order through a manufacturing company. The data in the figure are based on actual sample averages from a Midwest company. A typical order spends 5 days in the Order Entry Department before being released to production, then it takes 12 days for components to be fabricated, 9 days for assembly to be completed, and 8 days until the order is packed and shipped—for a total lead time of 34 days within the company. Figure 1.3 also shows the "touch time"—the shaded gray space in the rectangles—which is the time when someone is actually working on the job. (Again, these times are based on actual sample averages at the Midwest company.) You can see that touch time accounts for under 20 hours; so based on an 8-hour day, the touch time is less than 2.5 of the 34 days. The rest of the time is the "white space" in the rectangles, where nothing is happening to the job. Incidentally, this ratio is not unusual at all—from hundreds of projects at manufacturing companies, I have observed that touch time typically accounts for less than 5% of lead time, and in some cases even less than 1%.

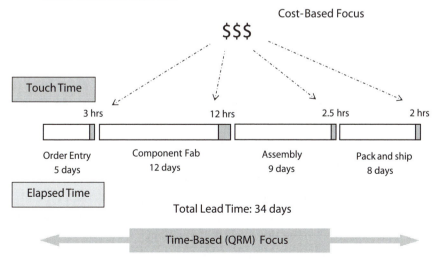

FIGURE 1.3
Difference between cost-based and QRM approaches.

Traditional cost-based approaches focus on reducing the touch time (gray space). Taking the company in Figure 1.3 as an example, in an attempt to reduce cost and be more efficient, management might target what appears to be the largest cost driver for this job, namely the 12 hours of labor spent in fabrication. An improvement team is formed comprising a machine operator, a tooling expert, and an industrial engineer. They study the fabrication operations and come up with new methods and tooling that reduce the fabrication time to 9 hours—a 25% reduction in labor cost for fabrication, and an apparently big success by traditional measures! But what effect does this improvement have on the lead time of the job? The 3-hour reduction is barely a dent in the 34-day lead time, and would not even be perceptible to customers.

In contrast, the QRM approach focuses on reducing the total lead time (gray space plus white space, from start to finish). This QRM approach usually leads to a very different focus on what to improve, and results in different management decisions compared with those that result from the cost-based approach. You will see specific examples of these differences throughout this book.

So a core concept in QRM is that you always keep the spotlight on lead time, or more precisely, on the reduction of lead time. In fact lead time reduction will drive everything: the understanding of your business, management decisions, and performance metrics. However, as soon as you pursue this line of thinking, a few questions arise:

- What exactly is "lead time"—more specifically, how is it defined in a precise way?
- Why should you focus primarily on reduction of lead time—can this focus be clearly justified for your business?
- How do you use lead time instead of cost as a primary driver for decision making and performance measurement?

Clearly, the answers to these questions will be critical for success of your approach: If your measure of lead time is ambiguous, it will result in mixed messages to the rest of the organization, or even manipulation in the way it is reported; if you are not completely clear about why you need to pursue lead time reduction, you will slide back into traditional cost-based decision making; and finally, if you go down the path of using lead time as a driver, you need mechanisms for translating this into specific actions. All of these issues are addressed by QRM principles and will be discussed in this book.

I will begin with the first question: what is "lead time"? This is not a trivial question. In a manufacturing enterprise, there are many different lead times, including:

- **External lead time:** The lead time perceived by customers
- **Internal lead time:** The time it takes for jobs to make their way through the organization
- **Quoted lead time:** The lead time that salespeople are currently quoting to customers
- **Planning lead time:** The value used for each routing step in the Material Requirements Planning (MRP) (or Enterprise Resource Planning [ERP]) system
- **Supplier lead time:** The time it takes to get material from suppliers

These are only a few; there are many other lead times in an enterprise. To support my statement that the preceding question was not trivial, look at the first two definitions of lead time, and consider the example of a midwestern axle manufacturer. This company supplies axles to farm equipment manufacturers. It takes the company 8 weeks to make a batch of axles, starting with bar stock and proceeding through multiple fabrication operations including heat treatment, plating, and finishing operations. This is the internal lead time in the preceding list. On the other hand, by keeping a stockpile of its finished axles, when this company gets an order from a customer it can fill the order and ship it out within 2 days. If the customer is within the Midwest as well, the order will arrive within another day. So the lead time perceived by the customer is 3 days. This is the external lead time in the preceding list. Hence the question for the QRM approach is: Do you count the lead time as 3 days or 8 weeks?

It gets more complicated. Suppose a line of axles is made from a special alloy with a 10-week lead time from a supplier. Normally, this company keeps raw-material inventory of this alloy, so it does not affect the company's internal operations. But this inventory costs money, plus if the company were to run out of raw material due to incorrect planning or unseen demand, then this lead time would affect the operations. So, should you or should you not include these 10 weeks in your lead time metric?

MANUFACTURING CRITICAL-PATH TIME (MCT)

As the QRM approach was being developed and refined, many of us working on the QRM theory struggled with these questions. Finally, in collaboration with several industry partners we came up with a metric that unifies all these different measures and clarifies the focus of QRM strategy. This lead time metric is called Manufacturing Critical-path Time (MCT), defined here as the typical amount of calendar time from when a customer creates an order, through the critical path, until the first piece of that order is delivered to the customer. From here on, the focus will always be on MCT as the metric.

Keep Data-Gathering Efforts Simple

I will now explain the definition of MCT. It begins by using the phrase "the typical amount." This is because MCT is intended to be a representative value that can be derived without going overboard with lots of data analysis. Due to real-world events that are common in manufacturing, each time an order flows through the organization the time it takes will vary. You might be put off using MCT if you think that detailed data-gathering and statistical techniques will be required to calculate this metric. In fact, the opposite is true. You should keep data-gathering efforts simple for two reasons:

- The purpose of MCT (in keeping with QRM philosophy) is to provide an estimate that is good enough to point you in the right direction—in the "Impact of MCT on Your Organization's Performance" section later in this chapter, you will see that large MCT values are also the major drivers of systemwide waste. Thus your aim is to get a ballpark estimate that highlights the biggest opportunities for improvement.
- A key insight after getting the value of MCT is to compare the amount of touch time ("gray space") with the total MCT value. As you saw in the example in Figure 1.3, the gray space usually comprises a small fraction (less than 5%) of the total time. There are typically large amounts of "white space" in the graph—surprising management and employees and motivating them to take corrective action using QRM methods. Thus it is not necessary that the MCT value be extremely accurate, as long as it demonstrates clearly the magnitude of the white space.

One of the strengths of the MCT metric is that a reasonable estimate will suffice. Thus it can be calculated easily and without too much organizational effort.

Measure in Calendar Time and Properly Quantify the Critical Path

The next item in the MCT definition is the term "calendar time." Essentially, MCT must be measured in real time and not the company's workdays, because calendar time is how delivery is viewed by customers. You also see in the definition that MCT starts with the creation of the order by the customer, since this is when the clock starts as far as the customer is concerned.

The next phrase in the definition—"through the critical path"—is key to the proper use of MCT for QRM purposes. "Critical path" for MCT is more than what this phrase typically means in project management. MCT not only quantifies the longest critical-path duration of order fulfillment activities including order processing, materials planning, scheduling, manufacturing, and logistics, but also quantifies waste in the system. Specifically, there are three important rules to be followed in calculating the critical path for MCT:

- **You must assume that all activities are completed "from scratch."** This means, for example, that if you normally fabricate components in-house, then prebuilt stocks of those components cannot be used to reduce the MCT value. You have to add in the time needed to make those components from scratch. (Common sense dictates that you should not worry about trivial components such as bolts, brackets, and the like. But with a wide range of components from simple to complex, how do you decide if a component is "trivial enough"? In Appendix A (on the enclosed CD) I will give you more details on how to calculate MCT, along with specific rules to help you decide which components should be included in the MCT metric.)
- **You must add in all the normal queuing, waiting, and move delays that jobs incur, and not use values for expedited (hot) jobs.** For example, consider the welding operation for a factory where components are fabricated, welded into subassemblies, and then assembled into finished products. For an urgent order, components can be expedited through welding in a day. However, for regular jobs, components

typically take a day to be moved from fabrication to welding. Then, because there are typically other jobs ahead of them, these components wait in queue for 3 days on average before they are moved into the welding booths; it takes another day for the welding to be completed. Finally, it usually takes another day for the welded subassemblies to be moved to the final assembly area. In calculating the MCT value, it is important that these typical moving and queuing times are accounted for in addition to the time for the operation itself. Also, you should try to use actual move and wait times, rather than using the theoretical ones in your MRP system or other planning system. If data for these actual times is not readily available, Appendix A (on the enclosed CD) gives you some simple ways to estimate these times—remember that for MCT calculation, reasonable estimates are good enough.

- **While in a manufacturing business prebuilt stocks are used to reduce lead time, in QRM on the other hand, time spent by material in any stage actually adds to the MCT value.** This is done in order to capture and quantify the total system waste, as I will illustrate in the following section. So if there are stocking points at any stage of the operation—raw material, work-in-process (WIP), and finished-goods materials—you need to add into the MCT value the amount of time that material spends waiting at these stocking points.

MCT takes the perspective of the first piece of an order; this is to ensure consistent measurement of the value regardless of order size. This is particularly important in terms of providing insights into improvement opportunities, as you will see in later chapters when I discuss batch-sizing trade-offs.

Note that MCT ends when the order is delivered to the customer's point of receipt. This implies that MCT includes logistics time, which is of particular interest with the growing emphasis on global sourcing. It is important to quantify the impact that logistics time has on a manufacturer's ability to respond to customers. Also, with long distances involved, costs associated with expediting orders can rapidly spiral out of control. When long logistics times are involved, then once an order has been shipped from a supplier it becomes very difficult, and sometimes impossible, to influence delivery time.

An MCT Example

In this section, I illustrate the use of MCT with an example that will help drive home how it is applied, as well as the insights obtained by use of this metric.

Consider Industrial Valves Corporation (IVC), a hypothetical company that makes small valves for industrial applications. IVC has a reputation for quick delivery of orders and promises customers that any order will be shipped from IVC within 2 days. IVC has a warehouse stocked with finished goods. When it receives an order from a customer, it takes 2 days to process the order, pick the valves needed, and pack and ship the order. Think about this for a minute: is the MCT value for IVC 2 days?

I hope you answered "No!" since this analysis didn't go through the critical path—the preceding times depended on the use of prebuilt components instead of doing things from scratch. So let me give you the next piece of information. IVC has a factory across the street from the warehouse, and when the warehouse runs low on stock for a particular valve, the lead time for the factory to deliver a batch of those valves is 4 days. So now, think about this a bit longer: is the MCT value 6 days (4 days for the factory and 2 days for the items in the previous paragraph)?

This time, your answer should be "it depends," because you need to look inside the factory. When you do, you find the operation shown in Figure 1.4. The factory has an assembly area, and when a replenishment order is received from the warehouse, components are picked from a stockroom and assembled into the desired valves. The lead time to get a batch of valves through assembly is typically 4 days—the value perceived by the warehouse. However, the components in the stockroom are made in a fabrication area of the factory, and the lead time for component fabrication is typically 7 days. Upon further investigation, you find that usually components spend 5 days in the stockroom before they are used in an assembly. Continuing your investigation, you also find that on average, a valve spends 11 days in the finished goods warehouse before being shipped to a customer. Let me summarize these steps shown in Figure 1.4, and

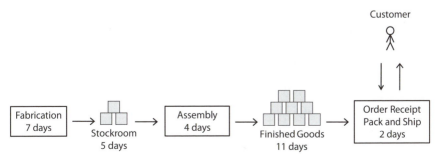

FIGURE 1.4
Overview of process steps at Industrial Valves Corporation.

then you can add them together: fabrication (7 days); stockroom (5 days); assembly (4 days); finished goods (11 days); order receipt, pack and ship (2 days)—this gives you a total of 29 days.

Here is a significant insight: The customer lead time of 2 days that IVC uses for its competitive edge is supported by a business process that is 29 days long. The difference between 2 and 29 should immediately be a huge red flag for management. Actually, I am still not done with calculating the full MCT value for IVC, but before continuing I will pause for some discussion.

The IVC example is typical of the insights obtained when the MCT metric is applied. As an example of this, I led a team that was tasked with studying the operations of several poorly performing suppliers to an OEM (original equipment manufacturer) in the construction industry. Along with those suppliers, the OEM gave us one of its best suppliers to use as a benchmark. We gathered data in order to evaluate the MCT of each of the suppliers, including the best one. The results were an eye-opener for both the OEM and the best supplier—this supplier's short lead time to the OEM was supported by an MCT that was 250% greater than the lead time! Now, you might well ask, if the OEM was happy with this supplier, then why does this matter? The answer, as I will show you more clearly in the following section, is that even though the OEM thought this was a good supplier, the MCT metric indicated that there was still a lot of room for improvement at the supplier. By applying QRM methods to make improvements in MCT at the supplier, the OEM can expect to see not only shorter lead times from this supplier, but also higher quality and lower costs—all of which will benefit both the OEM and the supplier.

Now I continue with the IVC example. There is still more to investigate in order to get the full MCT value. You need to look into additional processes and answer questions such as:

- **Information flow delays**: Are there additional delays associated with information transmitted from the customer to IVC, or within IVC's internal operations, such as a fax that sits in an "in" tray, or a job waiting for a scheduling decision?
- **Planning time**: How long does it take for planning processes that are used to determine that more parts are required for the stockroom and to release jobs to the fabrication area?
- **Raw-material stocks**: Is material spending a lot of time in stocking points even before manufacturing?

- **Supplier lead times**: What is the length of the process upstream of IVC, which may also involve multiple levels of suppliers?
- **Logistics time**: How long does it take for finished product to get from IVC to the customer?

As you can see, the full scope of the MCT measurement covers your whole business process as well as your supply and delivery chains. To help you measure MCT properly for your operation, I have provided you with a number of tips and detailed examples in Appendix A (see the enclosed CD). But if this seems too daunting—that applying MCT would require enormous amounts of data gathering about your operation as well as upstream and downstream processes—do not despair! You can begin the QRM journey by applying MCT to sections of your business at a time, and then expanding from there. Let me return to IVC as an example. You could start by measuring MCT just for the fabrication through assembly part of the operation (16 days, including the stockroom as shown in Figure 1.5) and focus on improving this with the QRM methods described throughout this book. Or, to give another example, you could start with the assembly through shipping part of the business (17 days, including the warehouse time, also see Figure 1.5). In Chapters 2, 4, and 5, I go deeper into how to choose where to start and how to determine the focus of your initial QRM project. As you measure and then improve this first segment

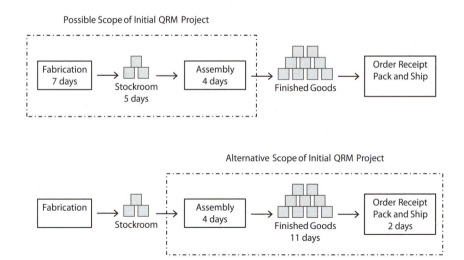

FIGURE 1.5
Examples showing limited scope of initial MCT data gathering and QRM project.

of the operation, you can then expand the scope of the MCT measurement and your QRM improvement projects. The main point is this: Although MCT can be a comprehensive metric that applies to your whole operation, you can start applying it in smaller segments so that you can get projects off the ground without having to wait for a huge data-gathering effort.

I would like to make two clarifications at this stage.

First, due to the way in which MCT was developed, the language in the definition is aimed at manufacturing and order fulfillment operations. Since the MCT concept is now being supported by many industry and government entities and has been adopted by hundreds of organizations, I want to keep the definition intact. However, later I will show you how we can interpret the definition to apply it to other areas of the organization including office operations, engineering, and new-product introduction.

Second, if you have been involved in recent Lean initiatives, MCT may appear to be the same as Value Stream Mapping (VSM). In fact, the two have many similarities, but they are not the same. For one fact, there are specific rules about applying MCT that differentiate it from VSM. But more important for you, as a manager, is that the whole idea of MCT is that it reduces the evaluation of your operation (or segment of your operation) to one number, thereby simplifying targets and clarifying goals for the whole team. If you start with an MCT of 28 days and after improvement projects you arrive at an MCT of 5 days, it is clear that your projects have been very successful! VSM is also a powerful tool, but the "current state" map in VSM has a lot of detail and it can be hard to get key insights on where the biggest opportunities lie. Similarly, in the "future state" map it is not immediately clear where improvements have been made. However, the tools are not in opposition to each other. If you are already using VSM, you will be pleased to hear that MCT and VSM complement each other and many organizations have used them together to help analyze and improve their operations. Appendix A (on the enclosed CD) provides additional details on these points.

Impact of MCT on Your Organization's Performance

Since I have now provided a well-defined measure of time, henceforth I will use the term "MCT" rather than "lead time" when I need a metric in relation to QRM projects. Note, however, that there are still many situations where the term "lead time" is appropriate and I will continue to use it in such cases. For example, I may need to refer to a specific lead time associated with conventional terminology, such as a planning lead time or a quoted lead time. Also, in several descriptions later in the book, I will continue to use "lead time" to denote the intuitive meaning of the term in order to make the description readable, but will always use MCT if I need to be precise about the concept involved.

So why should you, as an executive, consider using MCT as a primary metric for your organization? The IVC example gave you a glimpse of the answer to this, in that you discovered that a 2-day response time was being supported by a 29-day business process. But that is just the tip of the iceberg. Now I will show you in more depth why you should focus on MCT as a metric and on its reduction as a goal.

In order to do this, I am going to ask you to think about the following question: What are all the types of waste in your whole enterprise due to long MCTs? Let me clarify the question before you spend some time on it. I am not asking you what causes the long MCTs in your enterprise. Rather, I would like you to think about this "blue sky" situation, in order to capture what waste exists in your enterprise today.

What are all the things in place today that would be reduced or eliminated if your company's MCT were 90% shorter than it is today? More specifically, what are all the activities and tasks that are done today that could be reduced or eliminated? What are the investments in materials or resources that could be reduced or eliminated? (If your MCT were much shorter and these items could be reduced, this means they are truly waste in your enterprise today—they are there only because of your long MCT.) And what new opportunities would be available to your company that are not available now? (Again, these are also part of the waste today because your long lead times are resulting in wasted opportunities for your company.)

Let me help you start on this thought process. Suppose your company's MCT for a product today is 10 weeks. Suppose further that you woke up tomorrow and somehow, magically, your MCT was just 1 week. Imagine the functioning of this new organization, and as you do that, you will start to get insights such as, "Oh dear, I now realize that we have this whole set of procedures in place to help us manage the job flow during the 10 weeks, but if the job were to go in and out in a week we could eliminate all those activities and resources!" So this is an example of waste in your enterprise today due to long MCT, because if your MCT were shorter you would not need all those activities and resources. Similarly, in thinking about the last question in the preceding paragraph, you might say, "Oh yes, we have been trying to get into Market X with our products but have been unable to do so because our lead times are too long. We could gain 20% more sales if our lead times were much shorter." Although this item is an opportunity, it is also part of the waste today because your long MCT is resulting in a wasted opportunity for your company.

Now spend some time thinking about the answers to the preceding questions, and make a list of these wastes in relation to your particular enterprise. In fact, in setting the stage for QRM efforts I have found it useful to conduct a workshop where employees and managers get together and generate this list of wastes due to long MCT as a group exercise. You may find this to be a useful exercise at your company as well. After you have spent some time making your list (and please be sure to do this first), you can proceed to the following summary of items that are listed frequently by other companies when they engage in such a group exercise.

Enterprise-Wide Waste Due to Long MCT

The following are examples of activities and costs that are incurred today but would shrink or be eliminated if MCT were reduced substantially:

- Expediting of hot jobs or late orders requires systems, unplanned air freight, shop floor and office personnel to manage and execute the changes, even top-management time to negotiate priorities between multiple hot jobs
- Production meetings required to update priorities and change targets
- Overtime costs for trying to speed up late jobs
- Time spent by Sales, Planning, Scheduling, Purchasing, and other departments to develop forecasts and frequently update them
- WIP and finished goods holding costs and space usage
- Resources used to store and retrieve parts repeatedly during the long MCT, plus potential damage to parts due to the repeated handling
- Obsolescence of parts made to forecast and stocked but not used
- Quality problems not detected until much later, resulting in large amounts of rework or scrap
- Time to deal with delivery date and quantity changes, and with feature and scope creep (job specifications keep changing during the long MCT, constantly causing rework)
- Order cancellations or loss of sales to competition
- Sales time devoted to expediting and to explaining delays to customers

- Investment in complex computer systems and organizational systems required to manage this dynamic environment

Examples of opportunities that are lost because of long MCT include the following:

- Opportunities to gain market share by offering shorter lead times for current products
- Opportunities to beat the competition to market and gain market share through rapid introduction of new products with improved functionality

As you compare your list with this one, I'm sure you will see many items in common, but perhaps there are some eye-openers as well—items that did not occur to you but now that you see them you realize that there is more waste due to long MCT than you initially thought. Reduction in your MCT would reduce all of these items, resulting in a substantial impact on your enterprise including a significant reduction in overhead costs (most of the items fall in the category of overhead); an increase in employee productivity (people working on getting a job done instead of constantly redoing things); improvements in quality; generation of new sales opportunities; and many other benefits that you will see throughout this book.

In fact, let me provide more insight into the issue of overhead in the context of manufacturing companies and markets today. Figure 1.6 shows an analysis of part production volume that would be typical of a company

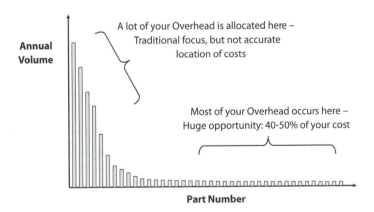

FIGURE 1.6
Where is your overhead, really?

that makes a large variety of products and/or custom products. The figure shows each part's annual production with the parts ranked by volume, starting with the highest volume parts. For such a company there are a few high-volume parts, but then there are a large number of low-volume, and even very-low-volume parts. The diagram shows only a small number of parts, but for companies that have many product options or custom-engineered products, the number of parts can be in the thousands or even tens of thousands. Further, many of those parts might be made in quantities of only one or two a year and possibly only once and never again. Now think about where your overhead is allocated by your accounting system versus where it really occurs. (Note: Some companies use other terms for overhead allocation, such as "absorption," "applied overhead," or "burden.")

In most manufacturing companies, overhead is still allocated using fairly simplistic rules based on direct-labor hours or machine hours. Since the high-volume parts consume a lot of these hours, a significant amount of overhead gets allocated to those parts. But that is not an accurate representation of where the overhead costs are actually occurring in the organization. Consider that the high-volume parts are the ones made daily or weekly; everyone knows how to make them and not much supervision is required; their production standards are known so their schedule is predictable; the supply chain has been set up and material arrives regularly; the quality systems are in place so quality is high; and so on. In contrast, the parts made once in a while need a lot of care and feeding by the whole organization: an engineer may need to modify a base design; a purchasing analyst needs to order specialty material; a new numerical control (NC) program has to be created; special inspection methods need to be devised for this item; and more. It is for these parts that most of the overhead costs are incurred by your company.

In fact I can quantify these differences. The high-volume parts might account for a lot of direct-labor costs, but as already mentioned, in a typical U.S. factory the total of all direct-labor costs is only around 10%. Thus, optimizing this section of the operation might impact only this 10%. On the other hand, overhead can account for 40% to 50% of the cost of goods sold, and as shown, most of this overhead occurs in support of the production of the lower volume parts. Now you can appreciate the power of the QRM approach. When you use QRM methods to reduce MCT, you achieve a huge reduction in overhead activities and costs. This is the strength of QRM—in companies that make a large variety of products with a large number of options or custom-engineered products, QRM has helped to reduce overhead costs by 30% or more. If you consider that overhead could be 50% of your cost and this portion could be reduced by 30%, that is a 15% reduction in the cost of goods sold. And the beauty is that this cost reduction does not come at the expense of other performance measures; quite the opposite in fact, because at the same time you achieve MCT reductions of 80% to 90% and huge improvements in quality!

Let me return to the part volume analysis shown in Figure 1.6. As you look to the future and think about the theater of competition—today's markets, described earlier, with modern technology as an enabler—you are definitely going to see more and more product variety, and more customization of products, a trend that is becoming known as mass customization. Thus it is all the more important that your company become adept at handling this variety of low-volume production in order to secure its future. QRM is a powerful tool to assist you in this effort.

IMPACT OF QRM—STANDARD COST PREDICTION VERSUS ACTUAL RESULTS

These arguments should be convincing enough for you to say "Let's do it!" and embark on adopting strategies to serve today's markets with high variety configured or custom products supplied with short lead times. But in trying to pursue such strategies, you will immediately face multiple obstacles. Some of these were pointed out via the QRM quiz earlier. However, the most insurmountable obstacle is often your accounting system. To see this, revisit Figure 1.3, which illustrated the progress of an order through a company. As pointed out there, traditional cost-based methods strive to reduce the gray space (the "touch time") in this figure, on the assumption that this will reduce product cost. QRM methods can be startlingly different. A QRM analysis might show that the MCT of 34 days in Figure 1.3 can be reduced to 5 days by implementing QRM methods—however it also turns out that implementing these recommendations will result in the gray space in Component Fabrication increasing from 12 hours to 14 hours, and the gray space in Assembly increasing from 2.5 hours to 3.5 hours. Now this will immediately draw all kinds of objections from management, because according to your accounting system these increases in gray space will result in large increases in your product cost. The opposition to the recommendations might be severe enough that your QRM efforts will be killed before they even begin!

Before I address this concern, let me give you insight into why QRM might recommend increases in gray space, in order to reduce the total MCT. This is a preview of the types of recommendations that QRM makes, and these and many more will be explained and justified in this book. This preview serves to alert you, early in this book, to the types of issues you will need to deal with as a manager driving QRM implementation.

In the Assembly area, let's say that today the assembly is done in three departments, each completing one step of the assembly. Each department operates in a manner so as to minimize the labor time per piece. This includes the way the department is laid out, the fact that large batches of parts are set up for one operation at a time, and the fact that employees are trained only in completing one step of the assembly as fast as possible. Although each piece is completed with minimal labor time, the department works on a batch of parts and then this batch queues up and waits to be moved to the next department. The QRM analysis recommends that a "QRM cell" be formed with employees who are cross-trained and provided with multiple tools so that they can complete all the steps in one area. (I will describe QRM Cells in detail in the next chapter.) However, since employees will now have to work on multiple steps, and use different tools and possibly also retrieve different components for assembly, they will take longer to complete the assembly of each part. On the other hand, since the batch won't queue and move between three departments, the batch as a whole will be completed in a matter of hours rather than days. So the touch time will increase a little, but the MCT will decrease substantially. But because the touch time increases and also because you will pay the cross-trained workers higher wages in view of their higher skills, if you apply overhead based on labor then the accounting system tells you that your costs will go up.

As another example, in the Fabrication area QRM might recommend running smaller batches through the machines. Since running smaller batches requires more setups, again the gray space will increase and the accounting system will tell you that your costs have gone up. On the other hand, in Chapter 3, you will understand how smaller batches can significantly reduce your MCT. A final example is that QRM recommends that you invest in spare capacity. Where a traditional study might suggest that a fabrication area can get by with five machine operators, QRM might suggest that you employ six operators. You will understand the reasons for this in Chapter 3 as well. Again, your costing system will tell you in no uncertain terms that this will increase your costs.

But think about this some more. If you increase your gray space by 3 hours, but your MCT is reduced by 30 days, as in the preceding example, did your costs really go up? What if, as a result of the MCT reduction, you can make some of your products entirely to order instead of to stock? As a result of this change, you can shut down one of your two warehouses, eliminating not only the costs of the inventory but also the costs associated with the building, the materials-handling people, the record keeping, obsolescence costs, and much more. (In fact, even if you don't shut down a whole warehouse, just modest reductions in materials handling might easily outweigh the increase in direct-labor costs.) It doesn't stop there. You have a team of planners, marketing people, salespersons, materials analysts, and manufacturing managers that meets regularly to discuss forecasts and make decisions on inventory and workforce capacity. All these meeting times can be eliminated, allowing people to use their time more productively. You also find that you now have more capacity on the shop floor because you were often making parts to forecast, and if those parts did not sell then that capacity had been used only to drive up your inventory costs. These and many other effects cumulate with the result that instead of your costs going up, you find that your costs go down significantly!

Accounting Systems Miss the Connection

So where did your accounting system make the mistake that resulted in the wrong prediction? The answer is simple. MCT is the sum of the gray space and the white space. Accounting systems simply do not identify a clear connection between the cost of the white space and specific products or activities. The cost of the white space goes into the general overhead pool where it is commingled with other costs and disconnected from its root causes. Then this overhead pool is applied across all products. Thus if you increase the gray space a little but reduce the white space a lot, the accounting system predicts only the impact of the increase in labor cost plus allocated overhead, but not the benefits of the white space reduction. The moral of the story: "The white space has a cost too! And most accounting systems do not directly connect the cost of the white space with root causes."

To drive this all home, let me remind you as to what really is the cost of the white space. In most companies, white space accounts for 95% to 99% of the MCT. And I have already asked you to think about all the costs of long MCT at your company. These costs are typically much, much higher than the few dollars represented by the gray space. For example, adding even 2,000 hours of labor in a year (one more person) might cost you only $50,000 for the year including benefits, but eliminating a warehouse could save you millions of dollars a year!

Let me explain some of these examples visually, to drive the point home even more vividly. Figure 1.7 shows three bars with their heights representing the total cost of a product. The first bar is the current cost, broken out into the three traditional components of standard cost: material, labor, and overhead. Let's say that this represents one of your current products, and a QRM analysis at your company recommends creation of a QRM cell with cross-trained labor. This might result in increase in gray space as well as in wages, as just explained. The second bar shows what your accounting system predicts, namely a large increase in total cost since the overhead allocated to this product also increases in proportion to the labor cost increase. On the other hand, the actual result with QRM is in the third bar, where the overhead has decreased significantly for reasons already explained, and so the total cost actually decreases. So not only do you have lower cost, but you also achieved a huge decrease in MCT and thus improved responsiveness to your customer!

The story doesn't stop here, it gets better. Many years of experience with QRM at hundreds of companies have shown that over a period of time

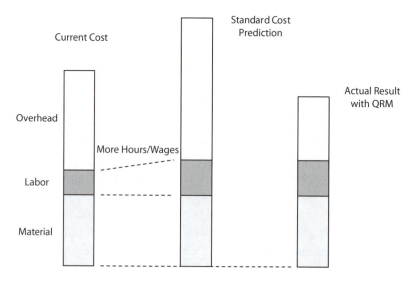

FIGURE 1.7
Impact of QRM cell: standard cost prediction versus actual result.

you will see additional improvements as shown in Figure 1.8. Let's start with the material component of the cost bar. QRM methods adopted in the supply chain (described in Chapter 4) have typically reduced material costs for companies by 15% to 20%. Second, as I will show in the next chapter, the organizational structure that results from QRM creates the opportunity for large improvements in productivity. So even though it appeared initially that it would require more labor to implement the QRM policies, over a period of time you find the increase in productivity means that you use less labor than before to make the same product. Finally, the overhead is reduced substantially. All of this results in the second bar in Figure 1.8, which is even lower than the last bar in Figure 1.7.

And it gets better still! There is yet more opportunity for improvement because there are other expenses in the enterprise that are not included in standard cost calculations. These are collectively known in accounting parlance as selling, general, and administrative (SG&A) expenses and include such items as marketing and sales expenses, accounting and general administration expenses, executive management, and other such costs. In addition there are research and development (R&D) expenses. I will put these together with SG&A to get a category that you can think of as SG&A/R&D expenses. I will make my point about these using Figure 1.9, which although simplistic in accounting terms, still serves to illustrate the point. (Note that for readability of the figure, I have simply labeled the combined SG&A/R&D category as SG&A in the figure.)

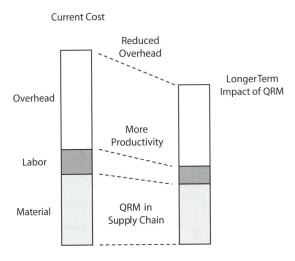

FIGURE 1.8
It gets better! The longer term impact of QRM.

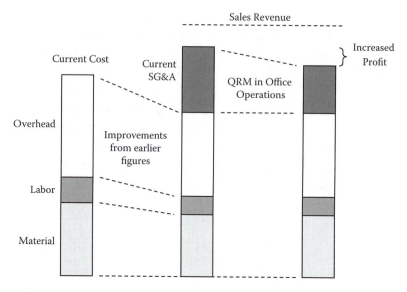

FIGURE 1.9
The impact of QRM on SG&A expenses and overall profit.

The first bar in Figure 1.9 again shows the current cost and its components. In the second bar, the lower three rectangles show the improved cost components that resulted in Figure 1.8. You can interpret the height of the bar up to the top of the white rectangle as the total cost of goods sold for the whole company. Then you add the current SG&A to this bar to get a view of the total expenses for the whole company. The horizontal line above it represents the total sales revenue. Hence the difference between the top of the second bar and the sales revenue is the current profit. In Chapter 4, I show you how you can apply QRM in office operations as well as in new-product development. The use of QRM methods in the office and in R&D, along with the fact that QRM reduces much of the administrative efforts in an organization, means that QRM results in substantial reductions in SG&A/R&D expenses as well. The net effect is a significant increase in profit as shown in the third bar in Figure 1.9.

Encouraging Time-Based Thinking throughout the Organization

The bar graphs in Figures 1.7, 1.8, and 1.9 illustrate the difference between traditional cost-based thinking and QRM's time-based thinking. This time-based thinking extends beyond shop floor decisions. To maximize the success of QRM methods, it is important that people in all areas of the enterprise engage in time-based thinking. I will illustrate this with an example for employees engaged in design engineering, using the Industrial Valves Corporation again. One of the components that IVC fabricates needs to be plated as part of its manufacturing operations. Since the company does not have a plating facility, IVC, located in the U.S. Midwest, sends the parts to a facility on the East Coast. (This is not an exaggeration. I visited a factory in Iowa that sends parts to Rhode Island for plating!) Because of the transportation costs involved as well as the long lead times at the plating supplier, IVC sends the parts for plating in large batches. These parts have a total MCT of 6 weeks. Of this, the in-house fabrication operations account for only 2 weeks, while the plating (including transportation and waiting times before and after the plating) accounts for 4 weeks.

An alert design engineer reviewing the product notices this fact, and after some research discovers that there is a new alloy on the market that would allow the component to be made without any plating at all, and still preserve the engineering properties needed for proper functioning of the part. This would reduce the MCT from 6 to 2 weeks, a 67% reduction. However, the alloy does cost more than the material currently being used, so when the engineer proposes this change it is shot down by management because the standard cost calculation shows that this will substantially increase the cost of the end products. This is illustrated by the first two bars in Figure 1.10. On the other hand, time-based thinking would make you examine the overhead costs that would be reduced. If the MCT were to be reduced from 6 to 2 weeks, you could eliminate a whole lot of planning, forecasting, inventory, obsolescence, and other costs that have been discussed in preceding examples. You might even change from making this component to forecast to being able to make it for each order, completely doing away with the forecasting activity altogether. These reductions might well be much greater than the increase in material cost, with the result of lower total cost as shown in the third bar in Figure 1.10. Plus IVC would now be more responsive to customers and demand changes.

You may well ask at this point, how do I know if the overhead reduction will be sufficiently large? One way to find out is to attempt to identify all the activities that would be reduced or eliminated and to quantify their cost impact on products. This is often not easy for support activities whose magnitude in relation to individual products is not clearly known. For example, you might have to estimate how much time a person in the Scheduling Department spends rescheduling and expediting a particular

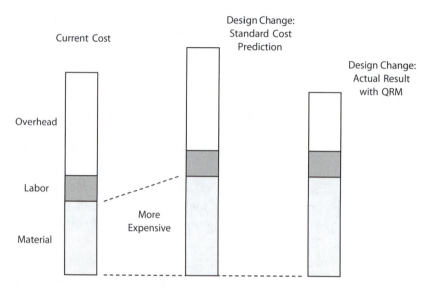

FIGURE 1.10

Example of impact of time-based thinking applied in design engineering.

line of products, and other such activities that have never really been measured before. A second way is to use some rules of thumb that I will explain later in this book, which make the task of prediction much simpler. The main point I would like to make at this stage is that the type of time-based thinking illustrated in Figure 1.10 should pervade the whole enterprise, and as people throughout the company engage in such exercises, the cumulative effects can be astounding.

RETHINKING THE "ON-TIME DELIVERY" METRIC

A significant indication that most manufacturing management does not engage in time-based thinking is the fact that very few companies do a good job of measuring any of their lead times with actual data. There may be anecdotal measures, or theoretical lead times used for planning, but little actual and accurate data is collected on a regular basis for assessing lead times or MCT. While some data may be collected on the shop floor, there is typically little or no data collected on job flows through the office. The only traditional metric that attempts to look at time is the "on-time delivery" measure, which reports the percentage of jobs that reach their destination (internal or external) on time when compared to the planned arrival time. Unfortunately, the only measure commonly used actually has a serious drawback. To see this let me revisit the fourth item in the QRM quiz in Figure 1.2: We must place great importance on "on-time" delivery performance by each of our departments, and by our suppliers.

I stated earlier that for success of lead time reduction efforts, each of the statements in the QRM quiz need to be answered "false." But what could possibly be wrong with emphasizing on-time delivery performance? In fact, almost every book on modern manufacturing discusses on-time delivery and states that it is a cornerstone of JIT and Lean programs. What I have observed, though, is quite different when it comes to MCT reduction as the goal.

Dysfunctional Impact of the On-Time Delivery Metric

While on-time performance is desirable as an outcome, the emphasis on it as a performance measure is dysfunctional. Instead of helping to reduce MCT, internal departments and external suppliers alike tend to pad their planned or quoted lead times so that their on-time deliveries look good. As an example, some years ago I observed the operation of a welding department that supplied components to final assembly. The supervisor of this department was measured by on-time delivery to final assembly. In addition to this measure was the pressure that if his welded components were late, they could hold up shipment of the final product, which was worth hundreds of thousands of dollars. As a result, the supervisor had, over the years, worked with the Planning Department at the company to give himself enough planned lead time in the MRP system. While in most cases the department could complete jobs within a 2-day lead time, there would be times where due to equipment failures, defective welds, or absent employees, the Welding Department could get backed up to over a week. So this supervisor had convinced the Planning Department to maintain a 2-week lead time for his operation in the MRP system. Moreover, the supervisor was always looking ahead in the schedule and if he thought his department would have a lull in its workload, he would start work on jobs way ahead of their planned start date, just so they would be finished well in time and his measure would look stellar.

So what did the on-time metric accomplish for this department? First, it resulted in an incentive for a manager to inflate planned lead times, thus institutionalizing a longer MCT in the enterprise. Second, it encouraged this manager to start jobs ahead of time, which meant that when they were finished early they would just "sit" and add to WIP costs and MCT values. Third, when jobs that were not yet needed were started, if a job that was needed urgently happened to arrive, it created a ripple effect of additional problems: The job that was already started might have had a long setup, and shop floor employees were reluctant to tear down this setup, so the needed job got delayed. Or the employees were forced to tear down the setup and work on the urgent job, but this meant they would have to redo the setup later thus adding an extra setup to their workload. Also, the job that was finished early took up floor space and might have had to be moved out of the way several times, perhaps needing a forklift truck for each move. Each of these moves increased the chance of damage to the parts, and so on.

Similar effects occur with suppliers to a company; knowing that they are being measured by on-time delivery metrics, they try to quote the longest lead time that they can get away with. This is particularly true when the supplier's experience is that the customer's forecasts are not reliable and the customer changes order quantities often. Then the padded lead time gives the supplier additional wiggle room to cope with these changes.

Such impacts of the on-time metric are not confined to the manufacturing part of the organization. A company that makes customized electronic products for the entertainment industry has project managers that work with their sales department. Their role is to put together and deliver a complex set of equipment and have it installed at the customer site. The project managers are measured by on-time completion of their installations. This company sells in a market where many companies compete based on quick delivery and installation. Yet several of the project managers confessed to me in private conversations that they do their best to pad their lead time quotes considerably, so that their on-time metric looks good at the end of the year.

In many cases though, things get worse. Individual departments padding planned lead times in an attempt to look good actually results in worse performance overall. When all the padded lead times are added up, the result is very long planned lead times for components and end items. This requires long-range forecasting and planning with all its pitfalls of excess inventory and WIP, forecast errors, hot jobs, and expediting. I will go into more detail about this in the next chapter. Suffice it to say that all these disruptions only make the performance suffer, and despite padded lead times and plenty of wiggle room in the schedule, organizations find their on-time delivery to the customer getting worse rather than better.

The QRM Approach to Improving Delivery Performance

So what is the solution? The QRM approach is simple and singular in its strategy: make MCT reduction the main performance measure, throughout your organization and also for your suppliers.

In Chapter 2, I show you how to design a performance measure that emphasizes MCT reduction, and in Chapter 4, I also discuss more carefully the issue of MCT in relation to the supply chain. As MCTs shrink throughout your enterprise and your supply chain, the dysfunctional effects of long MCTs will disappear, things will go as planned, and on-time performance will improve for everyone as a result. This is not just a conjecture; I have witnessed it again and again at companies implementing QRM. Table 1.1 shows results from four such companies. The second column shows the MCT reduction achieved, and the last column shows the dramatic improvements in on-time delivery.

I am not saying that you shouldn't strive for good on-time delivery. It's how you get there that is different in QRM. If you measure and reward everyone on their on-time delivery at each step of the chain, the result, as explained, is deteriorating on-time performance. If you motivate everyone to reduce MCT, the result is improved on-time performance.

SQUEEZING OUT TIME LEADS TO NUMEROUS IMPROVEMENTS

At the beginning of this chapter, I said that I would show you that time is a lot more money than most managers realize. In this chapter, you have seen the power of time. I can now summarize the first core concept of QRM in terminology I have established: Squeezing out time throughout your

TABLE 1.1

Impact of MCT Reduction on On-Time Performance

Company (Product Type)	% Reduction in MCT	% On-Time Performance (Before → After)
Hydraulic Motors	57	20 → 97
Seat Assemblies	80	40 → 95
Hydraulic Valves	93	40 → 98
Wiring Harnesses	94	43 → 99

enterprise (as measured by MCT) leads to numerous improvements, and your company becomes a formidable competitor.

Companies that have implemented QRM and cut their MCTs by 80% or more find that they can deliver to customers exactly the products that those customers want, customized to their needs. They can deliver these products faster than anyone else in the marketplace, often in a fraction of the lead time of their competitors, and with stellar on-time delivery performance. With the improvements resulting from QRM, these short-lead-time products do not cost more to make; in fact costs are reduced (see Table 1.2 for examples), so these companies can offer the customer shorter lead time and lower price. Or they can maintain the market price and increase their profit margins. Also, the short MCTs ensure higher quality so the company's product quality is second to none. In fact, MCT reduction results in more than just incremental improvements in quality— up to 100-fold reductions in defect rates have been experienced, as shown in Table 1.2. (Chapter 2 explains in more detail why such dramatic improvements occur in the QRM organization.) In addition, by implementing QRM in new-product introduction these companies continually beat the competition to market and gain market share by rapidly introducing new products with improved functionality. In short, these QRM companies leave no room for the competition to get in!

Now that you have understood the first core concept in QRM, the power of time—and in particular the importance of reducing MCT—in subsequent chapters I will show you how to actually accomplish this reduction throughout your enterprise and supply chain, as well as for new-product introduction. I will accomplish this by leading you through the other three core concepts in QRM which are: organization structure, system dynamics, and enterprise-wide application.

TABLE 1.2

Impact of MCT Reduction on Product Cost and Quality

Company (Product Type)	% Reduction in MCT	% Reduction in Product Cost	% Rework or Rejects (Before → After)
Hydraulic motors	57	13	1.5 → 0.05
Seat assemblies	80	16	5.0 → 0.05
Hydraulic valves	93	14	5.0 → 0.15
Wiring harnesses	94	20	0.3 → 0.05

2

Organizational Structure for Quick Response: QRM Cells, Teamwork, and Ownership

In this chapter, I show you the organization structure that will accomplish a 75%, 80%, or even 90% reduction in your Manufacturing Critical-path Time (MCT). In particular, I give you the four keys to the QRM organization, and you will also get to see, in more depth, the people side of QRM, which is equally important as the technical side.

I begin by reviewing the first management belief from the QRM quiz in Chapter 1. Traditional Belief #1 was that everyone will have to work faster, harder, and longer hours, in order to get jobs done in less time. This belief is based on the cost-based approach, which has a different focus than QRM's time-based approach. Essentially, the cost-based approach focuses on reducing the touch time (the "gray space" in Figure 1.3—see Chapter 1), which is typically less than 5% of the MCT. So the traditional belief won't make much impact on the goal of MCT reduction. Instead, the following is the QRM principle that must replace the first traditional belief. (Since I have now put in place a more precise concept of lead time, I clarify the goal by using MCT instead of lead time in the statement of the principle.)

The alternative QRM principle is this: Find whole new ways of completing a job, with a primary focus on minimizing MCT.

These "whole new ways" require major restructuring of your organization. Why? A first explanation is that you won't get 75% to 90% improvements by fine-tuning what you are doing today. A deeper explanation stems from the legacy of manufacturing enterprises. Organizations today are based on two principles: economies of scale and a focus on cost reduction.

RESPONSE TIME SPIRALS

Before I go further into these principles, let me show you some of the dysfunctional effects that result from this scale/cost thinking. I call these effects Response Time Spirals and, as you will see in this book, there are many of these dysfunctional spirals throughout the traditional enterprise. In this section, I introduce you to two of them—see if you recognize your own operation in one or both of these situations!

The Spiral for a Make-to-Stock Business

Consider a company that makes products to stock. This is typically done when the lead time to make a product greatly exceeds the customer expectations for lead time. For instance, let's take Acme Axles Corporation, a manufacturer of specialty axles for large construction and mining equipment. One of Acme's customers has a requirement that its suppliers must be able to "flex" their delivery schedule with 2 weeks' notice. However, Acme's time to produce those axles—starting from bar stock and going through all the machining, heat treating, plating, and assembly operations—is 8 weeks. So the only way that Acme can respond to schedule changes within 2 weeks is if it builds some of those axles ahead of time and keeps them in stock.

Now let me show you the Response Time Spiral that results for Acme or any similar company that makes products to stock. This spiral is shown in Figure 2.1. You will find it useful to follow the graphic in the figure as you read the explanation here. (Note that in this description I will revert to using the term "lead time" and not MCT because I will be describing the traditional planning approach that uses traditional notions of lead time.)

Acme has long lead times (that is, lead times that are far longer than the market will bear), hence its strategy is to build product ahead of time so that it is available in stock. This requires sales forecasts to decide how much of each product to build. Since Acme's planners know that the forecasts are far from perfect, based on past experience, the planners build in some additional safety stocks into the production schedule. The forecasts and safety stocks are not only for finished product, but also for fabricated components and subassemblies. In addition to these safety stocks (which account for a significant amount of extra production), some products and their components are made that do not sell as well as the forecast had

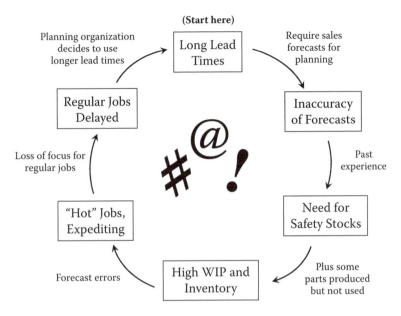

FIGURE 2.1
The Response Time Spiral for make-to-stock products.

predicted. Some components might even be part of the way through the factory when it is realized that they are not going to be needed as soon as expected, so their production is stopped and they are put aside. The net result of all these factors is that there is high finished-goods inventory as well as high work-in-process (WIP).

Now here comes the kicker. One of Acme's customers has introduced a new product that is selling far better than the customer had anticipated. Indeed, the customer's own forecasts were much too low, and based on these, Acme's forecasts for the required axles were far too low as well. As the customer's planning team rapidly revises its forecasts, it expects large increases in Acme's production schedule. At this point Acme's safety stock is nowhere near enough to satisfy these increases during the 8 weeks that it takes for Acme to produce axles. So Acme has to find a way to make these axles in 2 to 3 weeks. Everyone in manufacturing knows how this is done: this order becomes a "hot" job! Like an ambulance making its way through heavy traffic, this hot job is given priority through all the processes, and it makes it out of the factory in time to meet the customer's additional requirements. The customer is very happy with Acme and expresses its happiness with promises of more business. You would think that everyone at Acme would feel that the heroic efforts were worth the stress, except for one fact—this was not the only hot job. As you review Acme's operations, you find that the shop floor is cluttered with hot jobs. There are dozens of situations where forecasts were inaccurate and resulted in hot jobs for components, subassemblies, and completed axles.

As a result, the "regular" jobs (ones that are not hot) move at a snail's pace through the factory. Revisiting the ambulance analogy will make this clear. Imagine that you are waiting behind a long line of cars at a busy intersection, and just as the light turns green for your lane, an ambulance arrives and everyone in your lane has to move aside. You miss your chance and wait for the next time the light turns. Again, just as your turn comes, a police car arrives with its siren blaring! And so on. You (the regular job) keep being pushed aside while the ambulance and police car (the hot jobs) interrupt the flow and go ahead.

With all the expediting of hot jobs throughout the shop floor, the regular jobs keep getting behind schedule. Eventually Acme's planners notice that something is not right. A planner responsible for the finished inventory of a certain axle notices that there are frequent stockouts for that axle even though there was supposed to be safety stock. Upon investigation, the planner realizes that they were using an 8-week manufacturing lead time for that axle, and so they were releasing the work order to the shop floor 8 weeks ahead of when the completed axles had to arrive at the warehouse. Since this axle was not a hot job, it kept getting pushed aside and was actually taking 10 or 11 weeks to make it through the shop floor. After reviewing historical data for a number of shop orders for various axles, the planner decides that the 8-week lead time is no longer accurate for Acme's performance. "If we want to make sure that all these axles hit the warehouse on time, we really should release them 11 weeks ahead," the planner explains to the rest of the planning group. The data is convincing, so they agree and decide to use an 11-week lead time for all their axles.

So the lead time for Acme's factory has just spiraled up from 8 to 11 weeks. What happens next is not pretty either. Now Acme's planners have to work with sales to get forecasts that are 11 weeks out. Clearly, these forecasts are much less accurate than the 8-week ones, so they have to build in higher safety stocks as part of the plan. Also more parts are made that do not sell as predicted. Acme finds itself with even more inventory and WIP. But here comes the final insult. Instead of this new policy being helpful, after a few months there are even more delays due to hot jobs. Why? Because first, with looking farther out there are even greater forecast errors resulting in more hot jobs than before, and second, because during its 11-week sojourn on the floor, there are many more opportunities for a job to be interrupted than there were during an 8-week sojourn.

As these delays start to mount up, two years later these 11-week jobs are actually taking 13 or 14 weeks to get through. Our planner has moved to a different part of Acme, but another alert planner conducts a similar analysis and recommends that the 11-week lead time is not realistic; Acme should be using a 14-week lead time. The lead time has spiraled out once more.

Response Time Spirals tend to be insidious; they grow slowly, and there usually are personnel changes, so companies do not realize what is happening and keep adjusting to the new situation. The Acme story is no exaggeration; I have uncovered similar historical data at many companies. One aerospace equipment manufacturer went from a planned 6-month lead time for its products to 9 months, then to 12 months, then 16; and when I was asked to review the operations, they were at 24 months. The lead time had spiraled out over 10 years, so each change had not been that noticeable.

The Spiral for a Make-to-Order Business

If your business model appears to be different from Acme's, you might well protest: "We don't make our products to forecast. We make highly customized products, and in our business everything is made to order. So we don't have to worry about the spiral, right?"

Wrong! The spiral can infect make-to-order operations just as badly. Let's take the example of Beta Broilers Inc., a manufacturer of custom-designed commercial ovens used in factories that produce food products. Beta's ovens are typically engineered for each customer's specific application. Since Beta's products are customized, it cannot use forecasts to build products in advance. Instead, each oven is built to specific customer order. So instead of using a forecast for its planning, Beta uses a Master Schedule, which is essentially a list of the end products to be built along with the date each one should be shipped. This Master Schedule is then used—typically with a Material Requirements Planning (MRP) system—to drive the purchase and production of components and assemblies, timed so as to meet the ship dates. Now you might think that since Beta doesn't use forecasts, its operation should be better than Acme's, but you will see that the Master Schedule is actually not that different from a forecast.

Refer to Figure 2.2 as you read this description. Beta has long lead times for all its operations (for reasons I explain in the following section), so its

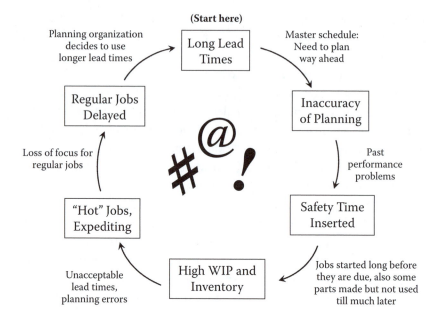

FIGURE 2.2
The Response Time Spiral for make-to-order products.

planners need to plan way ahead with the Master Schedule. This means the plans cannot be very accurate. Why? When a ship date has been set 4 months out, many things can happen in the interim: other important orders could be accepted; there might be production quality issues, equipment failures, or raw-material delivery problems; or the customer might request a change in the delivery date or even in the product design. Based on past experience, the planners insert "Safety Times" throughout the schedule.

For instance, consider one of the steps, which involves modifying a base design to customize an oven for a given application. This step needs about 8 hours of an engineer's time, but that doesn't mean that the planner schedules just one day for this job in the Engineering Department. Given that the Engineering Department has many other jobs to work on, the planner might initially allow one week for Engineering. However, after a year's worth of experience, this planner notices that jobs do not make it out of Engineering on time, and upon investigation finds that the engineers are often interrupted with crises such as warranty issues, production questions, and time-sensitive sales inquiries. So the planner decides to allow 2 weeks for engineering—with a 5-day workweek this converts to 10 days of lead time for Engineering. Thus you see that an 8-hour process now has 9 days of safety time added to it.

A similar process is repeated for the other steps that the job goes through, such as component fabrication operations, welding, heat treatment, subassembly, and final assembly. As a result, when these total times are added up, it is necessary to start jobs far ahead of their due date. Also, each job has components, subassemblies, and assemblies being made for it. This means that there are a large number of active jobs throughout the enterprise.

Now here comes the kicker (again!). Beta's lead times have become so long that its salespeople have trouble closing deals, and another dysfunctional effect is initiated: A salesperson quotes a 16-week lead time to a customer who then replies adamantly that this lead time is unacceptable and the customer will need to go with a competitor. As this is a large-dollar order, the salesperson calls back to the factory, talks to some people in operations, and negotiates a "special" lead time of 12 weeks for this customer, and is able to close the deal with the customer. Everyone should be happy to get this big order, right? Except that now this special lead time requires the job to be expedited through the operations and so—you got it!—it becomes a hot job. You know the rest of the story too, because we saw it at Acme: this is not the only hot job. Part of the reason for this is the sales issue, but in addition, the mere fact of having to plan way ahead guarantees that there will be inaccuracies in the plan and those miscalculations require jobs to be expedited to fix the problems. As more and more hot jobs interrupt the flow, the Planning Department realizes that the planned times for each step are not sufficiently long, and starts using longer planned lead times for each operation. Of course these longer planned times just result in more sales issues, more planning errors, and more hot jobs and a need for even longer planned times. And so the spiral grows ...

Roots of the Response Time Spirals

I'm sure you will agree that these spirals are greatly dysfunctional to a manufacturing business, but what is the connection between the spirals and the scale/cost thinking that I mentioned earlier? It all goes back about a century to pioneers such as Henry Ford and Frederick Taylor who developed many of the techniques of mass production and scientific management. They showed us that in order to minimize the cost of a product, you need to analyze the production process and break it down into lots of simple steps—such as, for Ford's early cars, putting a wheel on an axle or riveting the seat onto the floorboard—and each step could then be done by a specialized worker who was trained only on that single process. Since such persons did not need to have high skills, their wages could be very low. By suitably designing the production equipment as well as the jigs and fixtures, a sequence of such simple steps performed by low-skilled labor eventually resulted in a sophisticated product such as an automobile. These techniques were so successful that they brought down the cost of many products by an order of magnitude or more, putting many products such as cars within the reach of the common person, and ushering in the era of mass production and huge industrial growth.

This industrial model was based on making the same product over and over, but it was soon extended to situations where people made different but similar products. Consider the Charles Casings Company, which specializes in the machining of large housings and casings for products such as gearboxes, transmissions, and pumps. Even though Charles makes many different types of housings and casings, they all need turning on a lathe, they all need milling, they all need drilling, and so on. Thus the extension of the mass-production model to this situation was to create a group of people who focused only on turning, another group who did only milling, and similarly for the other processes. Each group consisted of specialized workers trained mainly on the set of skills needed for that function. These groups of people became "functional departments"—departments focused on a particular function (see the progression in Figure 2.3).

Continuing with the emphasis on reducing production costs, each department had a manager or supervisor whose job it was to make sure that this department operated with minimum cost. These managers soon realized

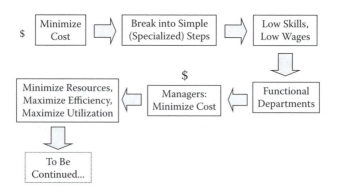

FIGURE 2.3
Roots of the Response Time Spiral (part 1).

that in order to minimize their costs, they needed to minimize the number of resources such as workers and machines. This was accomplished by trying to maximize the efficiency of each resource, as well as its utilization. While apparently trying to reduce cost, this approach however had a different effect as far as time was concerned. Let me illustrate this with an example.

To underscore the fact that this scale/cost mind-set extends beyond manufacturing to all parts of the enterprise, I will use an example from office operations and look into the Order Entry Department at Charles Casings. Customer orders arrive via mail, fax, or the Internet, and this department is responsible for entering the orders into Charles's computer-based planning systems. The department manager (let's call her Jill) is trying to minimize the departmental cost, so she has conducted an analysis of the workload arriving at the department each week. Figure 2.4 shows the results of this analysis: calendar weeks are along the horizontal axis, and the vertical axis represents the arriving workload in hours. The figure also displays two horizontal dotted lines: one indicates the peak workload during the analysis period and the other shows the average workload. The manager is trying to decide her staffing strategy. Assuming that one person provides about 40 hours of capacity per week, if Jill were to staff her department with four people she would have about 160 hours of capacity. The advantage of this strategy is that it would be enough capacity to meet the peak demand, and each week all the orders that arrived would be entered into the system.

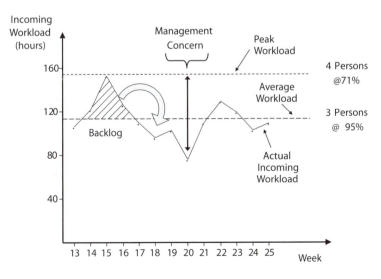

FIGURE 2.4
Effect of utilization-based strategies.

However, this staffing strategy has a major weak point for Jill, which is illustrated by looking at Week 20. During this week the demand is low and two of the employees have no work to do. If the president of the company were to walk into the department, he would notice this and be concerned that Jill was wasting the company's resources. Moreover, if the president noticed that this happened often (e.g., Weeks 18 and 24), he would eventually decide that Jill was not a good manager and didn't run a tight ship.

Since Jill has several years of experience as a manager, she anticipates this and instead she decides to have a staff of three people, giving her a capacity of 120 hours, or just over the average workload level. This means that in weeks such as 14, 15, and 16 there is more work arriving than can be handled, and these orders end up in a backlog queue. But this is exactly what Jill wants to happen, because when the demand drops during the following weeks this backlog fills up her staff's in baskets and makes sure that they have work to do. Now if the president happens to walk into the department, it is humming with activity and he walks out thinking, "Jill is a great manager—her people are always working so hard!"

What's the lesson here? It is that if your demand is somewhat unpredictable, so that it will go up and down from week to week, then the strategy of keeping people busy will require that you have a backlog. But think about this, who is in the backlog? Your customers! So in order to maximize the utilization of your people, you have made your customers wait. Jill could have gone with four people, each at an average utilization of 71%, but she went with three people with a utilization of about 95% each. Simply stated, here is the QRM lesson: The cost-based strategy of high utilization requires a backlog—but this is the opposite of being responsive to your customers!

I am not done with this chain of events yet—things get much worse. As part of the strategy of managing with fewer resources, managers try to ensure that each resource is used as efficiently as possible. To take a shop floor example now, consider a machine that takes two hours to change over from one product to the next. The supervisor of that department will want to minimize the time lost in changeovers, so he or she will encourage the machine operators to run jobs in large batches. This behavior is further encouraged by incentives for efficiency throughout the organization so that even the planners actively try to plan for parts to be made in large batches.

The picture at Charles Casings now looks like Figure 2.5. The company has been divided up into specialized functional departments, and each order needs to be processed through these departments. Each department has a backlog of work for reasons just explained. As shown in the figure, a typical

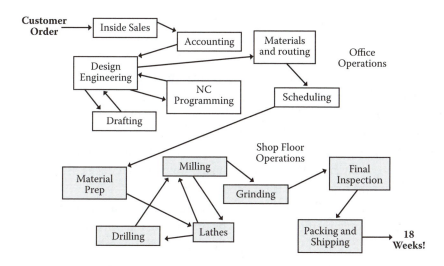

FIGURE 2.5
Resulting spaghetti flow and large backlogs at each step.

order arrives at Inside Sales, goes to Accounting, then to Design Engineering, then Drafting, back to Design Engineering, then NC Programming, and then back to Design Engineering again, over to Materials and Routing, then to Scheduling, which completes the office operations for this order and it is released to the shop floor. There the order starts in Material Preparation where raw castings are prepared for the machining operations, then it goes to the Lathes, then to Milling, then back to Lathes, on to Drilling, back to Milling, next to Grinding, then Final Inspection, and finally to Packing and Shipping from where it is dispatched on a truck.

If you were counting, this order just went through 18 steps! Now let's say each department manager operates with a "safety net" backlog of 1 week in order to make sure there is always enough work to keep people busy. This alone will account for 18 weeks of lead time, without even considering the processing time of the order in each department!

In fact, now also consider the time that jobs spend at each resource. These times are often long since jobs are processed in large batches for efficiency. Thus in addition to the backlog in each department, the transit times through departments are long. This also results in long feedback loops, so that quality suffers. To understand why this is, imagine that a cutting tool has been set incorrectly for the first Lathe operation, but this error is not caught until the Final Inspection step. Since this occurs 6 weeks later, during that time that bad tooling might have been used on many more jobs (up to 6 weeks' worth of jobs). Also, the incentive to make large batches means that it isn't just one or two pieces that need rework, but many huge batches of parts. So there is a lot of backtracking for rework, and some parts might have to be scrapped altogether and remade. This rework and remaking further delays jobs.

Since jobs are delayed for all these reasons, much organizational effort is now put into expediting. Figure 2.6 shows the conclusion of this progression. Charles Casings now has very long lead times and poor quality. One would hope that since the aim all along the way was to reduce costs, at least Charles could compete on its low cost, but to add insult to injury, Charles's management finds that costs are going through the roof. But why is this? Didn't the company minimize costs by organizing into specialized departments? Didn't it minimize costs by having the least number of resources in each department? The problem is that with the sequence of events just described, as well as the growing long lead times, all kinds of other costs are mounting up—remind yourself what these costs are by reviewing Chapter 1. The end result is that Charles has poor quality, long lead times, and high costs—the company is unable to compete on any of these three critical dimensions and is in grave danger of going out of business completely.

If you are wondering—"But this philosophy worked so well for Henry Ford and many other companies, so why is it a problem now?"—the answer is simple. Henry Ford designed his system to make the same product again and again, with very little variety, as demonstrated by his classic quote,

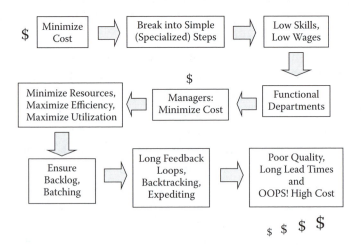

FIGURE 2.6
Roots of the Response Time Spiral (part 2).

"The customer can have any color he wants, as long as it is black!" Today's world, as explained in Chapter 1, has greatly increasing product variety and custom-engineered products, and this trend is only going to get more pronounced. The organizational structure that worked wonderfully for Henry Ford is no longer suited to this situation. You have to find a new structure that will keep your enterprise competitive in this environment.

FOUR STRUCTURAL CHANGES FOR QUICK RESPONSE

In order to achieve quick response in the face of varying and unpredictable demand, along with an environment of low-volume or customized products, you need to make four key changes to the structure of your organization (Figure 2.7):

- **From functional to cellular:** You must transform the organization of functional departments as described earlier into one comprised of cells—more specifically, QRM Cells. Although the cell concept has been in use for some time, QRM Cells extend this in several ways to achieve new levels of flexibility and performance; I elaborate on this in the following section.

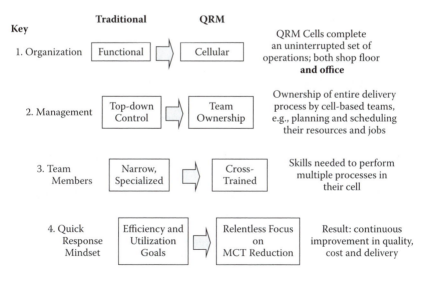

FIGURE 2.7
Organizational structure: four keys for quick response.

- **From top-down control to team ownership:** Instead of managers or supervisors controlling departments, QRM Cell teams manage themselves and have ownership of the entire delivery process within their cell.
- **From specialized, narrowly focused workers to a cross-trained workforce:** In contrast with the scientific management approach of having each person do one task as well as possible, you must create an organization where people are trained to perform multiple tasks. I will explain the numerous advantages of this organization, as well as how to decide on the level and scope of the cross-training in the "Key 3: Significant Investment in Cross-Training" section later in this chapter.
- **From efficiency/utilization goals to MCT reduction:** To support this new structure you must replace the traditional cost-based goals of efficiency and utilization with QRM's time-based goal, which is a relentless focus on MCT reduction. With the three previous changes coupled with this new focus, you will start to see amazing reductions in MCT. Further, even though you will have removed cost-based goals, you will see remarkable reductions in cost. You will also experience ongoing improvements in overall quality and delivery performance.

Key 1: Organize into QRM Cells

The concept of cellular manufacturing has been around for several decades. However, cells have typically been designed to be quite inflexible; they have linear flow with a fixed sequence of operations and prespecified "takt times" (fixed intervals) within which each step must be performed. QRM extends the cell concept in several ways.

QRM Cells are always designed around a Focused Target Market Segment, or FTMS. Hence, in order to explain how a QRM Cell is designed, I first need to explain the concept of FTMS. I will do so by using the situation at Charles Casings Company introduced earlier in this chapter.

Understanding Focused Target Market Segment (FTMS) through an Example

Charles Casings is losing business due to its spiraling lead times and has decided to use QRM as its strategy. It therefore begins to look at transforming its functional operation (Figure 2.5) into QRM Cells. Typically, you don't want to try to transform the whole company at once; you do this in stages. You begin by looking for a situation where there is a clear opportunity for benefit through lead time reduction. This is called a Target Market Segment. The company notices that, driven in part by rising fuel costs, there has been a surge in demand for aluminum casings because of their weight advantage over steel. The VP of Sales feels that Charles can gain a significant share of this growing market if the company can provide specialized casings within a short lead time. So the company decides to target these products for the first QRM Cell. Hence the Target Market Segment for Charles Casings' first QRM project is custom-machined aluminum casings.

To help you think through your own opportunities for QRM, note that "market" is used here in a generic sense—the customers for your QRM effort can be internal as well as external. An example of an internal customer could be a final assembly area that depends on various fabrication areas to feed it. If this final assembly area is often waiting for machined gears that are delayed in fabrication steps, then this is an example of an opportunity for a QRM project for an internal customer. The Target Market Segment in this case would involve gears needed by the final assembly line.

Returning to Charles's choice of aluminum casings, the next step is to refine and focus the Target Market Segment until you arrive at the Focused Target Market Segment, i.e., the FTMS that you are seeking to define. There are many ways to do this refinement and focusing and I will give you more pointers on this later. Here I illustrate the methodology with a typical approach that could be used for Charles Casings.

The approach begins with an initial analysis of demand for the aluminum casings based on their size—small, medium, and large (as defined by envelope sizes on Charles's machines). This analysis shows that among all aluminum casings, small casings account for about 15% of demand volume, medium casings account for 45%, and large casings account for the remaining 40%. Additional discussions bring out the fact that the large casings usually require the use of a very large milling machine. There is only one at Charles, and this machine is used by various other products as well. So management decides to exclude the large aluminum casings from the first QRM project. Next, it is found that the small casings require less machining and can be done on smaller machines than the medium casings. Grouping the small and medium casings together into a cell would mean that larger machines would often be used to work on a small casing, perhaps an overuse of a limited resource. Thus Charles's management narrows in on medium casings for the QRM project. A final concern is that some casings require specialized precision machining operations and there is only one precision milling machine at Charles. However, upon further investigation, it is found that such casings do not comprise a high proportion of orders. In fact, excluding these orders would reduce the percentage of remaining medium casings from 45% to 40% of all aluminum casings, not a significant reduction. Charles's management has now completed the process of focusing the original target market segment to arrive at the FTMS for their first QRM project. This FTMS is specified as "medium-size aluminum casings that do not require precision machining."

The preceding example does not imply that you always avoid complexity in the choice of the FTMS and "cherry-pick" the easy jobs for a QRM project, leaving the difficult jobs for the rest of the organization to handle. Rather, it means that different types of jobs may belong in different FTMSs. This project is just the first step and these more difficult jobs could be the subject of the next QRM project. In fact, mixing simple and complex jobs in the same flow is often the cause of poor performance in an organization. The FTMS approach helps you to create separate streams for jobs with differing complexity and characteristics.

Doing a good job in defining the FTMS is critical to the success of a QRM project. Depending on your products, processes, and the scope of your QRM project, there are many different ways to arrive at an FTMS, so I have devoted Appendix B (on the enclosed CD) to give you several pointers and other examples that will help you in accomplishing this process successfully for your own situation.

Having explained the concept of FTMS, I can now give you the precise definition of a QRM Cell.

Defining a QRM Cell

A QRM Cell is a set of dedicated, collocated, multifunctional resources selected so that this set can complete a sequence of operations for all jobs belonging to a specified FTMS. The set of resources includes a team of cross-trained people that has complete ownership of the cell's operation. The primary goal of a QRM Cell team is reduction of the cell's MCT. (Note that this definition is written in a way that enables it to be used not just in manufacturing, but in other areas of the organization as well. You will see how to apply the QRM Cell concept in other areas in Chapter 4. It is important for QRM implementation to have one unified definition that can be applied in all areas of your enterprise.)

QRM Cells differ in many ways from cells that have been traditionally implemented in industry. As one significant example of this, note that nowhere in this definition is there any mention of takt times in the design of the cell—I will go into more details on this as well as many other differences in the following section.

There are several important phrases used in the preceding definition. Each of these is carefully chosen and has a specific meaning.

- **Dedicated resources:** The resources assigned to a QRM Cell are fully dedicated to that cell. This means, for example, that if a milling machine is placed in the cell, it should be used only for jobs that are assigned to that cell (are in the FTMS) and not for other jobs. In particular, if management notices that this mill has some idle time, traditional thinking would suggest that they should find some other (non-FTMS) jobs that need milling operations and bring them to the mill to use up its idle time. In QRM this is an absolute "no-no"! By bringing in jobs that are not in the FTMS, you disrupt the cell's operations—for example, these jobs don't fit the pattern in the cell and create longer setups, which encourages more batching. There are even more significant reasons, however. Forcing non-FTMS jobs into the cell destroys what we call "cell integrity" and results in a chain of dysfunctional effects; I will talk about this more after I have explained additional concepts that are important to a QRM Cell.
- **Collocated resources:** The resources that form a QRM Cell must also be located in close proximity to each other in an area that is clearly demarcated as belonging to the cell. This will usually mean that machines and people must be physically moved to this new area. For machines, this may well involve some expense with foundations and utility hookups. For people, while moving to a different location in the same facility may not involve much expense, it is still difficult for them to leave their departments and coworkers and become part of an unknown and unproven entity. Thus in either case, whether machines or people are involved, there can be organizational resistance at all levels. Nevertheless, the benefits of collocation should not be underestimated and management should not compromise on this. First, just the act of physically moving the resources and creating the designated area of the QRM Cell sends a clear message to the

organization that management is committed to the QRM strategy and willing to invest what it takes to be successful. A second message from this is that the time for change is here; what you are effectively telling the employees is, "For us to succeed we can't go on with business as usual—we need to rethink our structure in order to remain competitive, and this is an important step in that direction."

- **Multifunctional resources:** The resources must be multifunctional (i.e., cover different functions). This may seem redundant in the definition, but I include it because I have seen many misconceived implementations of cells. The president of a company once took me on a tour of his shop floor, and while telling me that he really supported the cell concept he proudly showed me five CNC milling machines grouped together under a banner that said "Milling Cell"! The whole point of a QRM Cell is to move away from the functional organization, where a group of resources completes one function, to a new organization structure where a number of different functional steps get completed in one area. Keeping the word *multifunctional* in the definition helps to reinforce this point and hopefully, to prevent more mistaken implementations such as the "Milling Cell."

- **Complete a sequence of operations:** The idea here is that once a job arrives at the cell, it has a number of operations done on it before it leaves, and it should not have to go out and return to the cell repeatedly. Note that QRM Cells are more flexible than traditional cells. The sequence of operations can be different for different jobs in the FTMS and jobs can return to the same machine for a second or even third operation. But the point is that all these operations are done within the cell, and when the part leaves the cell it does not need to return. Since resources in a QRM Cell are dedicated, collocated, and must be able to complete a sequence of operations, it does take some analysis and brainstorming to decide which resources should be included in order to satisfy these criteria. Let's use the Charles Casings situation to walk through a typical analysis and brainstorming process.

Deciding Which Resources to Include in a QRM Cell: An Example

The first step in the process to decide on which resources to include is to look at the set of operations required for all the possible jobs in the chosen FTMS. The process for these casings starts with unpacking the raw castings and cleaning and preparing them for machining. Next there are several machining operations—horizontal milling, vertical milling, turning on a vertical turret lathe (VTL), deburring, and drilling—and these operations are done in varying sequences depending on the customized features for each job. In fact, some jobs require multiple visits to one or more machines. After this there are a few varied finishing operations, and finally packing and shipping.

Based on initial discussions it is decided that the unpacking, cleaning, and preparation operations will not be included in this first cell since these operations involve some large equipment as well as chemicals that require special handling due to EPA regulations. Initial analysis also showed that these operations account for less than 15% of the MCT for the FTMS jobs. Similarly, the various finishing operations are not included since they differ from job to job, and involve a multitude of different machines that would be too numerous to include in the cell. Packing and shipping requires a stock of many different materials and handling devices, and is also left to be done in the existing location. Again, these choices were reinforced by initial estimates that showed that all these operations did not contribute significantly to the MCT.

Management decides to form the first QRM Cell for all the remaining operations that are in the middle of the routing sequence. This means that it will need to have a horizontal mill, a vertical mill, a VTL, a deburring station, and a drill press. The machines chosen have an envelope size that is sufficient for the medium-size casings. Also, a rough capacity analysis based on demand projections shows that one of each type of machine should suffice, except in the case of the VTLs, where two will be needed. Decisions on capacity are a critical part of QRM and I will devote a significant part of Chapter 3 to this issue, so I will not go into more detail here. At this stage I will proceed with the decision that the cell will have two VTLs and one of each of the other types of machines.

QRM Cells Are More Flexible than Traditional Cells

In the description of Charles Casings' product flow, I noted that different types of casings can visit machines in varying sequences. This is not a problem for the Charles Casings cell; as I mentioned earlier, QRM Cells are designed to be more flexible than traditional cells, and in particular they do not need to have linear flow. As an example, Figures 2.8 and 2.9 show the routings of two different jobs going through the cell, and it is acceptable in a QRM cell to have flows that are not linear and that differ from job to job.

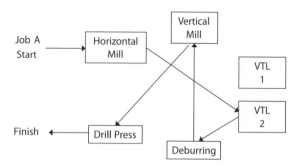

FIGURE 2.8
QRM Cells are flexible: routing for Job A in Charles Casings' QRM Cell.

In reviewing Figures 2.8 and 2.9, you are probably concerned about the complexity of managing these and possibly many other flows—in a traditional cell, jobs typically have a linear flow and the cell is designed around a takt time, which is a window of time during which each operation needs to be completed. This simplified flow and the takt time rule help to prevent bottlenecks. But for a QRM Cell with more general job flows and varying types of jobs, how do we ensure that there aren't unexpected bottlenecks and resulting job delays? QRM uses four strategies to address this issue. The first three are team ownership, cross-training, and the choice of metric, and are described in Keys 2, 3, and 4 later in this section. The fourth is the QRM approach to capacity planning, which is described in the next chapter. The combination of these four strategies enables the cell to operate effectively even in the face of multiple job types with different routings. This flexibility without degradation of performance is one of the strengths of QRM Cells.

The Charles Casings QRM Cell did not include in the cell all the operations needed to complete the FTMS products from start to finish—for

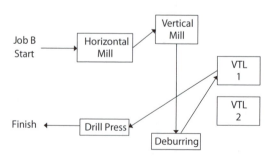

FIGURE 2.9
Routing for Job B in Charles Casings' QRM Cell.

example, some of the initial and finishing operations were excluded. An ideal cell would include all the operations from raw material to finished product, ready to ship—and in fact at the end of the chapter I will give you a case study of an actual cell that accomplished this. However, it is not always possible to include all operations in a cell—one obvious reason for this is if you make a very complex product, such as a large machine, there may be dozens or even hundreds of operations involved and the cell would become too unwieldy. In fact, there are many different ways of using smaller and more manageable cells to build complex products. One common approach is to create sets of cells—some for fabrication operations, some for subassemblies, some for final assembly, and so on. Each end product can then use differing combinations of cells to satisfy its production requirements. In Chapter 4, I explain how the flow between cells can be effectively coordinated using the QRM material control strategy called POLCA.

Another point to note is that in your first few QRM projects, as you are still thinking through the structure of your shop floor, it might not be possible to get all the operations for a product done in a cell—this is acceptable as long as the cell still covers a significant number of consecutive operations and makes a substantial impact on the product's MCT. However, you should continue to target more operations for this product in follow-up projects that will have the goal of either bringing those operations into the original cell, or creating new cells that include those operations. Eventually, you want your shop floor to consist entirely of QRM Cells.

Even when only a subset of operations is being considered for an FTMS, the goal of completing all those operations within the cell is still an ideal, and in reality there are many practicalities to be dealt with. For example, how do you deal with heat treatment or plating or painting, which are typically batch operations done using very large equipment? What if these operations need to be performed in between some of the operations that are being placed in the cell? It is indeed possible to get around some of these obstacles, and many different principles can be used. This takes some brainstorming and "out of the box" thinking by a cross-functional team in your organization. In Appendix C (on the enclosed CD) I give you a number of practical tips and examples that will help to stimulate such thinking if it is needed for your particular situation. I also describe a QRM technique called "time-slicing" that has been successfully used by organizations in the case where a large resource such as a heat treat furnace cannot be moved into a cell and needs to be shared by several cells.

Key 2: Team Ownership

The second key structural change is to move away from an organization where managers and supervisors tell people what to do, to one where teams have complete ownership of the processes within their cells. In a typical shop floor environment, a department supervisor assigns tasks to workers, decides on priorities among jobs, and moves people around if needed. On the other hand, in a QRM Cell, the team is given jobs along with expectations of when each one needs to be completed. However, how these jobs are completed is now entirely up to the team—the cell team is fully responsible for the operations within the cell. The team decides which job will be started next and who will run which machine, or who will help whom. The team decides if it is necessary to stop to solve a quality problem or to engage in a team meeting. Some teams even have the flexibility to stay late or leave early within parameters set by management—for example management may sanction up to 10% overtime, but allow the team to decide when to schedule it. Successful cell teams have even more responsibilities, as we will see in the case study that follows at the end of this chapter.

The power of ownership is frequently underestimated by management. When people are accountable but don't have a say in their operation, the result is frustration—or even apathy, as they see themselves as pawns in a bigger game over which they have no control. When people have accountability but are also given authority over their decisions, not only do they rise to the occasion, but they frequently exceed management's expectations. I will give you examples of this in a case study at the end of this chapter, as well as in Chapter 4.

This discussion also helps to explain further why resources within a cell need to be dedicated and why management must not destroy the cell integrity mentioned earlier. If management makes a habit of forcing non-FTMS jobs into the cell—say to increase the utilization of a given machine—the team loses ownership of the cell. Now the team can no longer plan how to use its resources with any certainty, and may not be able to meet its goals. The result is the frustration or even apathy already mentioned. In some cases it may seem difficult for management to justify dedicating an expensive or scarce resource to a cell. QRM helps you take a fresh approach to such decisions and gives you new insights that help in justifying these resources. I will discuss this further in Chapter 3. The main message here is that many of the benefits of QRM Cells stem from the ownership given to the team, and you should not lose sight of that fact and compromise this ownership during the cell's operation.

Key 3: Significant Investment in Cross-Training

There is already much awareness and discussion in industry of the need for cross-training. However, the importance of cross-training is underestimated, and the scope of cross-training is not strategically targeted. An obvious reason for cross-training cited by managers is that if each person knows only his or her process, and that person is sick or on vacation, then the whole cell operation comes to a halt. Another obvious reason is that the worker's job becomes more varied and thus more interesting and less monotonous. While both of these reasons are true, they are somewhat myopic and miss the big picture. In the QRM context, there are more significant reasons for cross-training and it is important for management to be aware of these so that it invests sufficiently in cross-training of the cell team.

- The first significant reason is that jobs in QRM Cells are highly varied in their needs, and so bottlenecks change from day to day and job to job. One job might require a lot of drilling, while another might require a lot of deburring. One job might require a lot of setup work on a VTL where it would be helpful if two people could work on it, while another job might run for two hours on a CNC mill without the need for an operator at all. Cross-training creates a flexible workforce that can move to allocate capacity wherever the bottlenecks are at a given moment. In other words, to effectively exploit strategic variability you must strategically invest in cross-training.
- A second significant reason for cross-training is that with modern automated or semiautomated machinery, you don't need one person for every machine in a cell. The Charles Casings QRM Cell with six machines (see Figure 2.8) might be staffed with only three people.
- A final significant reason for cross-training is that it results in long-term continuous improvement of unbelievable magnitudes. As one manager stated: "I thought that after a few initial improvements in the cell we wouldn't see any more, but we get improvements day after day, week after week, even though the cell has been in operation for over a year!" So why does this happen in the QRM Cell and not in the traditional organization? An example helps to see the answer.

Suppose Mike and Jeanette are two of the machinists working in the QRM Cell in Figure 2.8. Mike has traditionally been a vertical turret lathe (VTL) operator, while Jeanette has been running milling machines. Now they are cross-training each other in the cell. While Jeanette observes Mike doing a setup on the VTL, she notices that it takes Mike over 30 minutes of trial–and–error and adjustments to get a particular reference point accurately positioned for a casing. But she also knows that when the casing comes to her milling machine for the first operation, she has to line it up and at that moment she has accurate information on several reference surfaces for the part. So she comes up with an idea to mill two small slots on the casing in an area where they won't affect its functionality, and then they can use these slots to line up the casing when it arrives at the VTL. Jeanette and Mike try this idea out and sure enough, it enables Mike to line the part up in less than 5 minutes. They take this idea to the Engineering Department to make sure that the operation of the casings won't be affected, and it gets approved. As a result, a 30-minute setup has been reduced to 5 minutes, an 83% reduction in setup time. In the traditional organization, Jeanette would have been in the Milling Department in one corner of the factory, Mike would have been in the Lathe Department in another corner, and this interaction would never have occurred. Even if there was some effort to engage in cross-training in the traditional organization, the parts worked on in the Milling Department might have been so different than the parts being loaded on the VTL that no one would have thought of this idea. This also illustrates the power of the FTMS concept used in designing QRM Cells. As teams get more familiar with the types of jobs in the FTMS, it greatly increases the potential for them to come up with improvement ideas. In contrast, in a traditional functional department, each job can be so different from the next that you do not see any pattern to help you come up with improvement ideas.

Understanding the scope of cross-training is just as important as understanding the importance of it. Again, management is hesitant to invest in cross-training because it appears to take a lot of personnel time—for example to train a machine operator to become an expert on a new type of machine. If you have a skilled milling machine operator, it might take months of training to get that person certified to operate a VTL without assistance. However, training in the context of QRM Cells is more focused and achievable in a shorter time period. The key here is to note, once again, that a QRM Cell is designed to focus on jobs in a given FTMS. Thus, in the preceding example of machine operators, the goal of cross-training is not "get certified to be a VTL operator" but rather, "learn how to use the VTL only for the operations required by jobs in this FTMS." In the case of the cell for Charles Casings, the VTL may be needed only to machine a few types of internal and external diameters, for parts in a limited range of sizes, and always on aluminum and not other materials, so this limits the type of training needed to operate that machine. Thus, we have found that in QRM Cells cross-training proceeds at a much faster rate than expected, and people with limited initial skills are soon operating sophisticated machinery with confidence and with quality results.

A second aspect of the "scope of cross-training" question is: "Who should be trained on what first?" This is best answered by setting up a cross-training matrix. The rows are labeled with the team member names, and the columns are labeled with the skills needed in the cell in order to perform all the tasks that might be needed by jobs in the FTMS. You start by making an entry of either a "1" or a "2" on each square in the matrix where a team member has that skill: a "1" denotes that the member can perform that task at a satisfactory level, while a "2" denotes that the person has enough expertise on this skill to train others on it. If the team member does not have that skill or is not confident about it, you leave the square blank. After you have done this for the whole team, this matrix immediately gives you a visual evaluation of the skills in the team. In particular, you can see which team members have the least skills and also which skills have the fewest team members that can perform them. Based on this, you can now start designing your cross-training program. Your first cross-training goal should be to make sure that there are at least two team members who are competent in each skill. A second goal should be to create a training regimen for the less skilled team members. Complementing this, your third goal should be to make sure the more experienced team members have the responsibility to do the required cross-training. If the matrix highlights areas where no one on the team is sufficiently experienced or confident enough to train other people, then you should commit outside resources to the cell to conduct the necessary training. These four steps will get the cross-training under way quickly and on the right track. As these initial training goals are achieved and the team gets more experience with the cell organization and the FTMS jobs, it will have a good handle on what it needs and it can then be responsible to set subsequent training goals to improve its operation.

Key 4: Relentless Focus on MCT Reduction

The final key to the right structure is to have the right metrics in place. Companies create cells but still measure their performance using the traditional metrics. If a machine operator is being measured on efficiency or machine utilization, what incentive is there to take time out for team meetings, cross-training, or quality improvement? Instead this person will just "put blinders on" and concentrate on making parts and keeping the machine busy.

In QRM, the primary performance measure is unambiguous. The metric is the cell's MCT—in the two following sections, I will discuss further how to define MCT for a cell—and then the goal is to keep reducing its value. I showed you in Chapter 1 that as MCT is reduced, other key metrics get better. So, as long as the MCT value keeps going down, management should not be concerned about who is running which machine, whether the team is spending a lot of time in meetings, or whether a particular machine appears to be sitting idle from time to time. If the MCT is going down, the team must be doing something right. On the other hand, if the MCT value stalls or starts to go up, it is a signal to management that the team may need help, and then management can supply expertise and support to the team to help uncover problems and make the team more effective.

Understanding the QRM Number

This discussion brings up the point that not only do you need to measure MCT, but you need a metric that will effectively measure MCT reduction and also help to motivate teams. QRM does indeed provide such a measure: it is called the QRM Number. Although many companies stress the need to reduce lead time, few measure lead time accurately, as I pointed out in Chapter 1. Measuring lead time via MCT is a good start for an organization, but it is only the first step in implementing QRM metrics. Many of the benefits of QRM stem from MCT reduction, as was also pointed out in Chapter 1. It is well known in management theory that if you don't measure something, the message to the rest of the organization is that it does not matter. So how do you measure MCT reduction effectively, to ensure that it provides the right message? That is exactly what the QRM Number does.

Consider a newly formed cell. You measure its average MCT over a baseline period. Then you measure its MCT in the following periods. The QRM Number for each period is then defined by

$$\text{Current QRM Number} = \frac{\text{Base Period MCT}}{\text{Current Period MCT}} \times 100$$

Note in particular that the current MCT appears in the denominator. Now you may well ask, "Why bother to use this calculation? Why not just report the MCT values and use those numbers directly to evaluate whether the team is doing its job?" I will illustrate the answer with an example.

Table 2.1 shows data from a newly formed cell. Management has chosen the measurement period to be a calendar quarter (three months). During its first quarter of operation, the cell team achieves an average MCT of 12 days. During successive quarters, the team reduces its MCT to 10 days, then to 8 days, and finally to 7 days for the last quarter of the year, as shown in the second column of the table. Now I will calculate the QRM Number. This calculation is illustrated in the third column, and the resulting QRM Number is in the last column. You can see that the QRM Number starts at 100 (this is always the case, as is obvious from the definition), then increases to 120 for the second quarter, then to 150 for the third quarter, and it ends at 171 for the last quarter.

Using these data, I can now demonstrate that there are several advantages to using the QRM Number:

- When the team does its job effectively, the MCT value goes down, but the QRM Number goes up (see Figure 2.10). It is well known in the science of performance measurement that people react more positively to a graph going up than to a graph going down. In other words, if the desired performance results in an increasing number this will be more motivating to the team, and that is exactly what the QRM Number accomplishes.
- When the team takes two days out of its MCT in the second quarter, it gets 20 "points" (as measured by the increase in the QRM Number

TABLE 2.1

Example of Applying the QRM Number

Calendar Quarter	Average MCT for Cell	Details of Calculation	QRM Number
1. Jan–Mar	12 days	(12/12) × 100	100
2. Apr–Jun	10 days	(12/10) × 100	120
3. Jul–Sep	8 days	(12/8) × 100	150
4. Oct–Dec	7 days	(12/7) × 100	171

in the last column). Then, when it takes another two days out in the third quarter, it gets 30 points. Looking at the MCT values alone, there is an equal numerical achievement in both quarters. However, the QRM Number rewards the team more for the third-quarter effort. This is entirely appropriate for two reasons. First, with most improvement efforts there is usually some "low-hanging fruit" that you can pursue right away and which gives quick results, but then it gets harder to find improvement opportunities. Second, in terms of the relative magnitudes involved, squeezing 2 days out of 10 is harder than squeezing 2 out of 12. The values of the QRM Number recognize both these facts.

- In the final quarter the team manages to squeeze only one day out of its MCT, but it still gets 21 points—more points than it got for the second-quarter effort when it squeezed two days out. The QRM Number is designed to recognize the fact that as more and more improvements are implemented, it gets increasingly harder to find ways to reduce the MCT. In fact, if you were to just plot the MCT value, the graph would start to flatten out when this occurs, as can be seen in the MCT graph in the left half of Figure 2.10. On the other hand, as a result of the mathematical properties of the ratio used in its calculation, the QRM Number is designed so that it will continue to rise with significant slope even for small reductions in MCT (see the graph in the right half of the figure). Thus the QRM Number continues to motivate teams even when MCT reduction becomes more difficult.

- The QRM Number also provides a "level playing field" where teams across the organization can be compared and can engage in friendly competition. Let's say you have implemented three QRM Cells: one in fabrication with an initial MCT of 27 days, another in assembly with an initial MCT of 9 days, and the third, an office

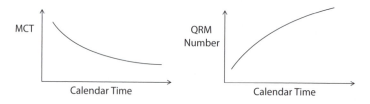

FIGURE 2.10
The QRM Number motivates teams to pursue MCT reduction.

cell to complete all the processes (for a chosen FTMS) from order receipt to release of a job to manufacturing, and which has an initial MCT of 5 days. All three cells will start with a QRM Number of 100. Even though each team starts with a very different MCT, and each is working with different types of processes, over the next few months as you observe the three QRM Numbers you will immediately know which teams are being successful and which ones need help. Also, use of the QRM Number is not restricted to one cell at a time; you can use it for a collection of cells, for sections of your enterprise, or for your whole enterprise. For example, you could track the average MCT for a whole factory, which may consist of multiple cells, and then plot the QRM Number for the factory as whole. In this way you can evaluate improvement at the factory level and even compare the performance of different factories in your organization.

- The QRM Number can also be used for supplier evaluation and supplier improvement, and helps to bring in a time-based measurement instead of just using the traditional cost-based supplier metrics. I will discuss this further in Chapter 4.

Ensuring Proper Application of the QRM Number

To ensure proper application of the QRM Number and to prevent potential frustration of team members, a few issues need to be resolved ahead of time.

First, the start and end points of the MCT for a given QRM Cell should be clearly demarcated—in other words, it should be clear when "the clock starts ticking" for this team, and also when it stops ticking. For example, the clock could start when the team has possession of both the material for a job as well as a work order authorizing the beginning of operations on the job. It could stop when the team delivers the job out of the cell and to the next operation.

Second, the clock should tick for this team only when it truly has ownership of that period of time. For instance, if the team needs to stop work on a part because of an issue with porosity of the casting being machined, and the team is waiting for engineering to make a determination of how to proceed with this job, then that period of time should not be allocated to the team. Specifically, the clock should stop while this issue is being resolved. From an implementation point of view, it is not always easy to start and stop the measurement. One way to do this would be to measure the full MCT and also record the length of time that the team is waiting for a decision (or other such situations), and then subtract these values at the end. In either case, however the MCT measurement is implemented, the team must feel that it has ownership of the segments where it is being measured, or else the metric will result in frustration rather than motivation. A corollary to this is that when the clock stops ticking for a team, it should start ticking for someone else! After all, from the customer's point of view if a job is late it doesn't matter that it wasn't the team's responsibility—if the team no longer has ownership, someone else needs to have ownership so the job keeps moving. In the preceding example of the casting quality issue being reviewed by engineering, there should also be pressure on engineering to resolve this issue quickly.

Don't let common sense be overrun with rules for QRM Number calculation! Use simple common sense to check what incentives you are creating with the QRM Number before you implement it. Here is an example of a pitfall. You implement an MCT calculation for a QRM Cell that includes a stockpile of machined components that are made by the cell and sit in the cell waiting for final assembly to request them. The cell team soon realizes that if it "bleeds down" this stock, then its MCT will look better. However, after it does so, there are times when it runs out of machined components and holds up final assembly. So what is the solution here? There are several possible ways to tackle this. One is that the cell team's MCT should not include the stockpile. The stockpile is the result of the planners releasing jobs in anticipation of assembly's needs and the MCT for this pile could be made the responsibility of the Planning Department. Another solution is to use an MCT measure from the beginning of the cell and through final assembly; this way if the cell holds up assembly the total MCT number looks worse, and the cell and final assembly need to work together to reduce their overall MCT. In similar fashion, prior to implementing it you should apply a "common sense test" to your suggested MCT measure for a team and its resulting QRM Number.

Some thought should be given to the units by which MCT is being calculated. A simple example serves to illustrate this point. Suppose one job of 20 pieces is completed with an MCT of 11 days, and the next job of 2 pieces is completed with an MCT of 3 days. If we compute the average by jobs, then the average MCT is $(11 + 3)/2$ or 7 days. However, if we calculate the MCT by pieces, then 20 pieces had an MCT of 11 days, and 2 pieces had an MCT of 3 days. Now the average is $(20 \times 11 + 2 \times 3)/22$ or about 10 days. So which is right, 7 days or 10 days? Since there is a considerable difference here, use of the incorrect value could provide the wrong incentive to the team or frustrate team members if they felt they were being treated unfairly, or both. The answer as to which calculation to use can be arrived at simply by looking at your overall goals. For instance, if each job represents a specific customer order, and your goal is to reduce lead times for orders, then measuring MCT by job is appropriate, and the value of 7 days would be used. On the other hand, if these parts are being made to stock and individual pieces will be sent to customers later, and your goal is to reduce total WIP and overall material Flow Times in your system, then weighting the MCT by piece would be a good way to go, and the average MCT of 10 days is the value to use. Similarly, you can think through your own situation. To make your task easier, my suggestion is: "Don't sweat the details! Go after the big picture." Keep in mind that the goal is not to know the exact MCT value but rather, through use of the QRM Number, to motivate its reduction. So if your measurement period is long enough that the average profile of jobs from period to period is reasonably similar, then any bias in the way you measure MCT will remain roughly the same from period to period, and the QRM Number will still reasonably reflect improvements in performance. Remain open to refining the MCT calculation as you gain experience with using it in your particular situation.

HARNESSING THE POWER OF THE FOUR STRUCTURAL KEYS

The set of changes described here goes far beyond what most manufacturing companies typically have done when trying to improve their operations. Although many companies have put in cells, they have not complemented them with other changes described, so they haven't exploited the full power of this organizational structure. Most cells today are based on takt time calculations and linear flow, which means they don't work for varying job types and are not flexible. Also, companies create cells but don't give them ownership—they still have supervisors micromanaging the operations. They put together teams but don't understand the importance of cross-training and limit their investment in it. And finally, they put in cells but measure people with utilization and efficiency metrics. It is no wonder that there has been so much discussion on why cells are not as successful as they are touted to be!

QRM overcomes these issues by making sure that the cell structure is complemented with other key changes. The concept of the QRM Cell, which begins by identifying and focusing on a properly chosen FTMS, and then combines a flexible cell structure with teamwork, ownership, and cross-training, and finally supports all this with the right metric, achieves incredible results. MCT and WIP reductions of 75% to 80% are often achieved, and some companies have seen 90% to 95% reductions as well. There are dramatic improvements in quality. Floor space reductions of 30% to 50% are realized—or conversely, companies can grow their business by 50% to 100% without requiring more space. Productivity improvements of 50% or more have been reported, and in some cases even 100% improvements (doubling of the output by a team!) have been reported. And the impact on the people is amazing, too. The organizational structure consisting of QRM Cells and the other keys described here boosts morale and improves employee attitude and satisfaction, creating a workforce that is enthusiastic, loyal, and committed to continuous improvement for the long-term benefit of the enterprise. All these points are illustrated by the following case study.

National Oilwell Varco (NOV) is the world's largest manufacturer of automated oil and gas well-drilling and pipe-handling equipment. Most of NOV's products are engineered to order. This case study is from the NOV factory in Orange, California. Products made in NOV-Orange include top drives (very large motors mounted at the top of the rig to turn the drilling pipes), and racking, stacking, and conveying equipment to handle the pipes. A few years ago, NOV-Orange was facing increasing demand for its products, but at the same time its long lead time and late delivery record were creating customer dissatisfaction and also opening the door to competitors who were eating away at NOV's market share. Management at NOV-Orange had been reviewing various manufacturing improvement strategies and felt that lean manufacturing was not well suited to their highly customized and low-volume business. They manufactured 60,000 different parts annually, and very few were made in high quantities; in fact the average lot size was under four. Around that time, Tom Becker, chief metallurgist at NOV-Orange, read my first book on Quick Response Manufacturing, and felt that it fit well with their manufacturing environment as well as their goals. He convinced management to explore putting in a QRM Cell to see how well QRM methods would work at NOV-Orange.

After some initial brainstorming, NOV-Orange selected two product families as the FTMS for this first cell. The families consisted of the following two product types:

- Internal blow out preventer (IBOP): This is a ball valve used to close off the bore of the drill pipe from the high down-hole pressures sometimes encountered in drilling operations. This product requires both machining and assembly operations, as well as specialized inspection processes. The machining involves mostly CNC lathes and mills including a combination lathe/mill machine. There is also some drilling: the valve body is cross-drilled for the actuators. There are many variations of this valve depending on the customer application; for example, the outer diameter may be straight, splined, or shouldered, or a combination of the three depending on other external functions to be performed. The assembly involves 29 internal components such as a ball, seats, springs, O-rings, and seals.
- Drilling sub: A length of pipe used to space tools within the drill string, to change the thread form of following connections, or to serve as a wear point and protect more-expensive tools. This product also involves similar machining operations as the IBOP.

These two products were selected because they both had long lead times (70 to 80 days) and sales were being lost to the competition. In addition, they required similar processes and were relatively self-contained; i.e., the products did not need operations from other parts of the factory. This choice of FTMS illustrates the point that because of their flexibility, QRM Cells can be formed around very different product types, as long as those products use the same collection of resources.

Management then set up an implementation team whose goal was to design the cell and implement it. The team was recruited from all the key functional areas, specifically: Manufacturing, Manufacturing Engineering, Production, Planning, Purchasing, Human Resources, and Accounting. The team's tasks were to come up with an initial design of the cell and the designated area for it, use projections of before/after metrics to justify the financial investments needed, recruit the cell operators and train them, move the needed machines into the cell, launch the cell, and support it until it was operating successfully.

In order to recruit the cell operators, the team posted bold and colorful flyers on the bulletin boards, and presented the cell as an exciting career opportunity. Workers from many different areas applied, and finally five were chosen. Interestingly, although the cell involved a lot of machining and assembly operations, not all five operators had machining/assembly background: one was a forklift operator working in the warehouse, and another was an inspector. There was considerable skepticism from some in the company as to whether these people would be able to learn the skills needed for the cell, but they were chosen because during the interviews they impressed the implementation team with their attitude, their enthusiasm for learning more skills, as well as their willingness to engage in team building and teamwork. In fact, eventually the warehouseman became as good a machinist as any of the others, and also assumed the role of team leader! This illustrates the point that management often underestimates the extent to which cross-training can be conducted, or underestimates the ability and eagerness of shop floor people to learn new skills.

The QRM Cell was implemented in 2001. Before stating the results, it is eye-opening to list the set of tasks that the team took over. There were, of course, the production tasks: starting from raw castings or bar stock, the team did all the machining and assembly. In addition, though, the team also performed a number of nonmanufacturing tasks, often called "indirect" tasks. They did all the inspection. They also took care of packing and shipping for their products. They set their work schedules within parameters set by management. They were even given responsibility beyond the shop floor functions—they could order materials from suppliers and set due dates for customer deliveries. On the human resource side, the key metric used by management to measure the team was the QRM Number, and to achieve their goal the team members were allowed to choose their own leader and do their own performance reviews.

This example underscores the extent to which ownership can be developed in a QRM Cell. And what was the impact of the QRM Cell along with the remaining QRM concepts of ownership, cross-training, and the right metric? Over the next two years, the team proceeded to reduce the MCT of these products from 75 days to 4 days! In addition, due to a combination of MCT reduction (with all its benefits listed in Chapter 1), plus process improvements by the team, as well as the team taking over some indirect functions, a recosting of the products showed that the team had also reduced the overall cost of those products by over 30%.

The lead time, financial, and people results from NOV's first QRM Cell were so impressive that top management approved several hundred thousand dollars of capital for additional QRM Cells to be implemented. (Since many of the machines in the Orange factory are very big, moving them would require a lot of resources.) In 2002 five cells were implemented, bringing about 20% of the overall shop load into cells, and by the end of 2002 the cumulative effects of the QRM program had resulted in savings of over $2 million—many times more than the amount spent in implementation. Over the next few years additional cells were implemented, and the Orange facility now operates with over a dozen cells. By 2005, the continuing positive results of QRM at Orange convinced NOV's Vice President of Global Manufacturing Strategy, Greg Renfro, to roll QRM out to other NOV facilities around the world. As stated by Greg Renfro, "QRM and the management of 'time' have been central to our ability to ramp up production and meet the demands of our market. As the market dynamics change, it will continue to be an integral part of reducing product costs, improving quality and shortening lead-times."

3

Understanding and Exploiting System Dynamics Principles

In Chapter 2, I showed you how to structure your organization in order to reduce your MCT. This new structure using QRM Cells is critical to QRM implementation; however, it alone will not necessarily ensure success. This structure needs to be supported by several other pillars of QRM, which will be discussed in this and the next chapter. To illustrate the need for these additional supporting structures, let me give you a few examples of companies that approached me seeking help with their ineffective implementations of cells:

- A manufacturer of specialized transmissions converted its entire operation to cells—several fabrication cells for components, and multiple final-assembly cells for various types of transmissions—and yet the company's quoted lead time to customers was 4 to 6 months. Furthermore, even with these long lead times it was still unable to achieve better than 40% on-time delivery!
- Engineers at a fabricator of aircraft engine parts put in a cell for a particular line of parts. Based on their cell design and their calculations, they expected a lead time of under 5 days for those parts. Instead, the lead time after the cell became operational was over 35 days.
- A manufacturer of medical devices had installed cells for most of its product lines, and the cells had dedicated equipment and operators. Yet the typical touch time within a cell was around 1% of the cell's lead time, and these lead times stretched to over a month even for cells making small and relatively simple devices.

These examples underscore the point that simply installing cells will not guarantee short lead times, or more precisely stated, short MCT. The cells need to be complemented with other management policies. In this chapter I will show you how system dynamics impacts your MCT, and how to exploit this understanding to reduce your MCT substantially. In particular, you will gain insight into how interactions between machines, people, and products impact your MCT. As a result, you will rethink your capacity-planning approaches (e.g., machine and labor utilization), lot-sizing policies, and other related decisions, to realize systemwide benefits. The use of system dynamics principles to reduce MCT is unique to QRM—other manufacturing management approaches do not explain or exploit this powerful methodology; they either base their system designs on simplistic assumptions, or else ignore this issue altogether. Yet as you will see, the insights from system dynamics are very powerful and when exploited they enable substantial reductions in MCT.

I will begin my explanation of system dynamics principles by revisiting the second management belief from the QRM quiz in Chapter 1: to get jobs out fast, we must keep our machines and people busy all the time (**Traditional Belief #2**).

As I explain in Chapter 2, this belief stems from the cost-based approach, which drives managers to maximize the utilization of resources, in order to minimize the number of resources required. Understanding basic system dynamics principles will, however, give us a new way of thinking about resource utilizations.

I will motivate our discussion with a typical situation that arises in the creation of QRM Cells. It is important that resources are dedicated to cells and cell integrity is preserved. Dedicating resources can, however, pose a problem when management has a traditional cost-based mind-set, because these resources may not necessarily be utilized all the time. Consider the example of the Charles Casings QRM Cell in Chapter 2. Suppose that for the subset of casings that will go through this cell, the amount of machining time needed on the Vertical Mill is much less than the time needed on the other machines. During the design of the cell, rough capacity calculations show that while the other machines will be utilized around 80% to 85%, the Vertical Mill will be used only around 40% of the time. Now this is a computer-controlled machine that costs around $450,000, and during a review of the cell proposal when a few senior managers see the 40% utilization number, they balk at the decision to put this machine in the cell. As one of the managers puts it: "We can't justify spending $450K on a machine that is only going to run 40% of the time!" So they decide that instead of buying a Vertical Mill to put in the cell, the cell will send parts for vertical milling to a machine in another area of the factory. We know from the previous chapter that this destroys cell integrity. At the same time, you are probably thinking, "This concept of 'cell integrity' sounds too ideal and not really practical—I too could not justify dedicating an expensive resource to a cell if that resource is used less than half the time!" So is it indeed, too much of an ideal, or is it indeed practical? I will lead you to the answer via a parable!

THE PARABLE OF THE LANDING GEAR

Joseph, a senior executive at a manufacturing company, is looking for ways to improve the company's financial performance, and decides to benchmark a few other industries to see if he can get some new ideas from those industries. As part of his efforts, Joseph picks the airline industry. Joseph knows that this industry operates with very expensive assets, so he decides to study the airline industry's approach to asset utilization. To do this, Joseph decides to take a flight from Boston to San Francisco.

As he boards the plane in Boston, Joseph starts a stopwatch ticking, and at the moment that he disembarks in San Francisco, he stops the stopwatch. He looks at it, and it shows a total sojourn time of 5:50 (5 hours and 50 minutes). This isn't the end of the measurements though. To help with his study of asset utilization, Joseph also carried with him a second stopwatch. When he boarded the plane in Boston, he also started the second stopwatch. Then, after the plane took off he listened carefully, and when he heard the landing gear being retracted (with the "thump" that is familiar to frequent flyers) he turned off the second stopwatch. As the plane approached San Francisco, he started listening carefully again. When he heard the whoosh-ing sound of the air on the landing gear as it was lowered, he started up the second stopwatch again. Finally, as he stepped off the plane he turned off the second stopwatch as well. This stopwatch now showed that the two time periods measured on this watch totaled up to 70 minutes.

Joseph now analyzed these times. The total time that the plane was deployed in carrying him was 350 minutes. During this time, the landing gear was in use for 70 minutes—or 20% of the time. Joseph now looked up the cost of the landing gear for the aircraft that carried him. The result astonished him, and he thought: "That $8 million landing gear only had a 20% utilization—they need to redesign their airplane to get a better utilization of their landing gear! Obviously I'm not going to learn much from the airline industry!"

So what is the moral of this story? I'm sure you thought, "It's absurd to measure the utilization of the landing gear!" And yet we often do the same thing in manufacturing companies without realizing it. Let's examine the two situations. The landing gear is part of a total system (the aircraft). The goal of the system is to deliver the passengers to their destination quickly and safely. Without the landing gear, this system cannot operate properly. The percentage utilization of the landing gear is not relevant to this goal. Similarly, let us consider the QRM Cell at Charles Casings. The Vertical Mill is part of this total system (the cell) whose goal is to deliver casings to customers quickly. Without the Vertical Mill, the cell will not be able to accomplish its goal. So why do manufacturing executives get so worried about the utilization of this machine? It is true that at the end of the day we need to turn a profit, and it is also true that you need to be careful how much you invest in a system in order to ensure that profit. So the correct question is not "What is the utilization of these machines," but rather, "What is the cost of this total system, and what is the return we expect to get from it?"

As an example, suppose the total investment in the cell is around $1.4 million, and it is estimated that the increased sales, reduced inventories, and other reductions in overhead costs will amount to an increase in profit of around $650,000 per year. Then you can expect a payback in about two years. After that you will continue to accrue the additional profit. In addition, you will have created a base of impressed customers, gain a positive reputation, and possibly pick up market share in other products too. With all these benefits, does it really matter if the Vertical Mill is only 40% utilized? Let's consider the alternative: You don't give the cell this mill. Then the cell is forced to get that operation done elsewhere, it does not reduce the lead time of casings enough to make an impression in the market, and the results are marginal at best.

To summarize, I am not saying that you should throw money away just to create a cell. What I am saying is that you should evaluate the feasibility of the cell as a total system. If it makes financial sense, then go ahead and implement it. If it doesn't, then you need to rethink the design of the cell, or even rethink the entire FTMS and go after a different opportunity. But if the cell makes sense, then do not micromanage the resource utilizations based on traditional management metrics—remember the lesson of the landing gear!

Another caveat here—if initial calculations show that the cell does not make financial sense, don't lose heart. There are many ways to improve on the initial ideas for the cell in order to make it feasible—these are described in Appendix C (on the enclosed CD) along with several practical examples.

THE PITFALL OF HIGH UTILIZATION

It would seem to make sense that in order to minimize the cost of all your resources, you should ensure that each resource is used as much as possible so that you are not wasting that resource. Then why is it bad to insist on high utilization? I gave you a preview of the answer in Chapter 2, where you saw the chain of events that resulted. Now I will go deeper into this issue.

I'll begin with examples from our personal lives, so you can see that my belief about utilization is not so unusual.

- You go to a major airport in the middle of the day and get checked in and through security in a matter of minutes. But arrive at the same airport around 5 p.m., and it could take you over an hour to get through these same processes.
- When you go to your supermarket on a regular weekday, you can get through the checkout in 5 minutes. But go to the same store a day or two before Thanksgiving, and it might take you half an hour to get through the line.
- You arrive at Chicago's O'Hare airport at 11 a.m. and catch a taxi that gets you to downtown Chicago in 20 minutes. The next time you arrive at 8 a.m., but now with the rush-hour traffic it takes you an hour and 20 minutes to get downtown!

You experience these situations in your personal life where you see that as resources get busy your waiting times increase—and not just by a small amount, but by leaps and bounds. Five minutes becomes half an hour, and 20 minutes becomes 80 or more! So why should you assume that factories are any different? As you push the utilizations of your resources higher and higher, you create greatly increasing waiting times for jobs—the opposite of the quick response that you are trying to achieve. In this chapter I will give you more insight into this phenomenon so you can better understand the trade-offs involved and make improved decisions for your enterprise.

Earlier I restated **Traditional Belief #2,** which is to ensure that your machines and your people are always busy. The principle that replaces this belief is quite different: strategically plan for spare capacity—the planned loading of your resources should be kept under 85% or even under 75% of their capacity (**QRM Principle #2**).

Your first reaction to this is bound to be: "We can't afford to do this! Our costs will be much higher than our competition that is using fewer resources." Initially this appears to be the case. For example, if you operate an area with five machines running at 80% of capacity, perhaps your competition could get the same production with only four machines running at 100%, and thus have lower costs. Traditional thinking would leave you to believe that must be the case. However, in this chapter I will show you that through a better understanding of system dynamics principles, combined with QRM's deeper understanding of MCT-related costs, you could actually have lower overall costs even when you plan for only 80% capacity utilization.

So why do you need any spare capacity at all? Why can't you operate with exactly the right amount of capacity to meet demand, and hence not waste any resources? The answer is contained in just one word: *variability*. In a perfect world, orders would arrive exactly according to plan, and each job would run on each machine for the precise amount of time that the engineers had calculated. In the real world, however, demand can vary a lot from week to week or even day to day, jobs can run longer than expected, a setup might be much harder than anticipated, material may not arrive on time, there could be quality problems and rework, and so on—any manufacturing professional could add many more examples to this list. Most executives understand this, but they don't understand the strong interplay between variability and utilization, and they definitely underestimate the enormous resulting impact of both of these on MCT. Conversely, they don't realize the significant difference that a small investment in spare capacity can make. I will now elaborate on these points.

Understanding the Magnifying Effect of Utilization

Thus far I've given you some anecdotes and examples to make you think more about the issues of utilization and variability. Now I'm going to give you more precise quantitative relationships that will give you a deeper understanding of this topic and the trade-offs involved. These relationships are derived from a branch of system dynamics theory, more specifically called queuing theory. Don't worry; I will keep the description elementary with only the simplest of mathematical formulas! Before proceeding to the relationships, however, I need to precisely define two concepts that I will use in this chapter.

Clarifying "Utilization"

The first concept to clarify is the QRM definition of utilization. For manufacturing managers "utilization" of a machine typically refers only to the proportion of time the machine is actually running (making parts). However, for proper decision making and trade-offs about capacity, we need a broader definition of utilization. In QRM, utilization is the ratio of the total time that the machine is occupied for any task (including the time it is unavailable due to maintenance) to the total time the factory (or that area) is scheduled to work. As an example, let's say a factory is scheduled to work 8 hours a day, 20 days a month, for a total 160 hours of total scheduled time. During this time, a particular CNC lathe is making parts ("in cycle") for a total of 104 hours and it is in setup for a total of 26 hours. It undergoes preventative maintenance for 3 hours. Also, once during this month it breaks down unexpectedly and it is down for a total of 11 hours before it is back up and running again (this includes the time it is waiting for a maintenance person to show up plus the time it takes to fix the machine). Adding all these times give you $104 + 26 + 3 + 11 = 144$ hours. In the traditional manufacturing definition, this machine has a utilization of 104/160 or only 65%. However, in the QRM definition, this machine has a utilization of 144/160 or 90%. This difference is one of the factors critical to your decision making.

Another way to understand the QRM definition is to "back into" the value of utilization by starting with the opposite question: What percentage of the time was this machine actually available to start an unexpected job if it had arrived at the machine? This tells you the true spare capacity at that machine. Subtracting this percentage from 100% gives you the QRM utilization. In the preceding example, there were only 16 hours during the month when this machine could have taken on extra work. This gives you a spare capacity of 16/160 or 10%. Subtracting this from 100% gives the answer of 90% utilization as before.

In fact, this alternative calculation method has the benefit of putting the focus on spare capacity instead of utilization. This is an important strategic decision in QRM as I will show you in the two following sections.

The preceding example explained how to calculate the QRM utilization for a machine, but the same rules apply when the resource is a person. For example, consider an operator working on assembling electrical products. The QRM calculation of utilization should include all the time used in the assembly tasks, plus time used for picking of parts, material handling, and setting up her workstation, as well as breaks and lunches, meetings, and even the typical amounts of vacation and sick days. Once again, the best way to confirm that the QRM definition has included all the significant times is to "back into" the value of utilization, by starting with the opposite question: What percentage of the time was she actually available to start an unexpected job if it had arrived at her station?

Clarifying "Flow Time"

The second concept I need to introduce is that of Flow Time. Imagine a job arriving at a resource. Since resources in a factory (people or machines) are busy most of the time, arriving jobs usually wait in a queue until their turn comes up. I define the Flow Time of a job arriving at a resource as the average time that it takes for that resource to finish other work that may be ahead of this job, start working on this job and finally to complete it. In other words, if you send a job to this resource, then on average, how long do you need to wait before this job will be completed and can go on to the next resource that it needs?

At this point you may be frustrated with having to learn yet another definition that has to do with time—after all, I have already discussed various notions of lead time and even developed a formal definition of time in the QRM context, namely MCT. So why do we need another one? The answer lies in the insight from Chapter 1 that time spent working on a job accounts for only a small fraction of its MCT—most of the time is spent waiting. This waiting can occur for many reasons such as waiting for material to arrive from a supplier, waiting for information from a customer, and so on, but a significant amount of the total waiting time in a manufacturing enterprise is waiting for resources to be available. The definition of Flow Time will allow me to focus specifically on this component of MCT and to make precise statements about it in this chapter. In turn, through a better understanding of this component you will gain insights into how to reduce it significantly, with a resulting significant reduction of MCT as well.

Putting It All Together

Now that you are armed with the QRM definitions of utilization and Flow Time, I can show you the enormous impact that the utilization value has on Flow Time, and as a consequence, on MCT. When a job goes to any resource in the factory, the total time it spends at that resource is the sum of queue time (the time spent in line, waiting for the resource to be available) plus the time it takes for the resource to work on the job (including the setup/changeover time). As just discussed, the time spent working on a job accounts for only a small fraction of its MCT—most of the time is spent waiting—so it is important to understand how to reduce this time. If you express utilization as a decimal number with value u (for example, for 90% utilization, u would have the value of 0.9), then the theory of system dynamics tells you the magnifying effect of utilization on queue times at resources:

$$M = \textit{Magnifying Effect of Utilization} = \frac{u}{1 - u}$$

Here I'm using the letter M as shorthand to denote the value of this "Magnifying Effect of Utilization." So what does this formula tell you? It shows how your queue times will blow up as you try to push your utilizations higher. If a resource has a utilization of 75% ($u = 0.75$), then M has the value 0.75/0.25 or 3. However, if that same resource has a utilization of 90%, then M has the value 0.9/0.1 or 9—just a 15% increase in utilization has tripled the value of M. What does this mean? The values of M are proportional to the queue times in each case—hence the ratio of M values is also the ratio of queue times you will see at that resource. For example, if during a month when a CNC lathe has a utilization of 75%, arriving jobs typically wait in queue for 3 days to get on the lathe, then during another month when the utilization is pushed to 90%, the typical queue time will jump up to 9 days. While 6 additional days may sound bad but not terrible, this is just the tip of the iceberg; the worst is yet to come. At this point, even small miscalculations in capacity, or any other disturbances (e.g., hot jobs, or machine breakdowns), can now cause an enormous increase in queue times. Let's say that between hot jobs and other workload estimation errors, the lathe's utilization is actually pushed up to 95%. The value of M catapults all the way up to 0.95/0.05 = 19! So jobs arriving at this lathe will now wait 19 days on average before they even begin to be processed.

If you look at the formula for M, you can see where this is going. As you push utilization closer to 100% (or 1.0), the denominator approaches 0, and the value of M literally blows up. So I wasn't kidding when I said that utilization has an enormous impact on MCT. Figure 3.1 provides a visual summary of this behavior, and also helps to contrast the cost-based view of utilization with the time-based one that I am presenting here.

The Miraculous Effect of Spare Capacity

Let me return to a statement I made earlier, namely that it is insightful to view your decisions in terms of spare capacity rather than utilization. By rewriting the formula for M, I will show you why this is so. Let s denote the spare capacity at a resource as a proportion of total capacity. Expressed as a percentage this means that if the utilization of a resource is 90%, then its spare capacity is 10%. In the following formula I express s as a decimal, just as I did with u. In this case $s = 1 - u$. (So in the preceding example of 90% utilization, $u = 0.9$ and $s = 0.1$). With this definition of s, I can now rephrase the formula for the magnifying effect of utilization as:

$$M = Miraculous\ Effect\ of\ Spare\ Capacity = \frac{1-s}{s}$$

Expressed this way, you see that spare capacity is beneficial in two ways. First, it appears in the denominator, so it rapidly diminishes the value of M through division. For example, if you increase your spare capacity from

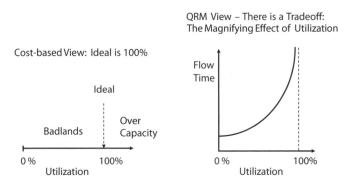

FIGURE 3.1
Cost-based versus QRM views of resource utilization.

10% to 20%, the denominator alone will account for cutting waiting times in half. Second, the 1 − *s* in the formula means that the numerator gets reduced as spare capacity is increased. In the instance just mentioned, with 10% spare capacity the numerator has the value 0.9, while with 20% spare capacity its value drops to 0.8. While this effect is not as pronounced as the denominator, it still helps to reduce waiting times. Putting these two effects together you see that increasing spare capacity from 10% to 20% means that *M* drops from 9 to 4, a 55% reduction. In other words, by adding only 10% of spare capacity at a resource, you have reduced waiting time at that resource by 55%. Now you can appreciate why I call it the "Miraculous Effect of Spare Capacity"!

Once again, it helps to see this effect visually. Figure 3.2 shows the impact of spare capacity on Flow Time. The graph there is the same as the one on the right in Figure 3.1. The arrows in Figure 3.2 highlight the principle that when you are operating at high utilization (i.e., very little spare capacity), a small investment in spare capacity (depicted by the horizontal arrow) results in a large reduction in Flow Time (as seen from the vertical arrow).

Impact of Variability

Now that you've seen the impact of utilization, let me explain the impact of variability on Flow Time. In manufacturing, one usually associates variability with dimensional variances in parts, such as variations in the

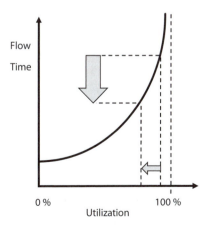

FIGURE 3.2
Miraculous effect of spare capacity.

machined diameter of a hole or variations in its location. However, in the QRM context, the concept of variability is used in relation to time. Specifically, there are two types of time-related variability that impact Flow Time. The first is variability in arrival times of jobs to the resource. I will explain this concept intuitively. Suppose that a new job arrives at a work center approximately every 4 hours; in this case there is very little variability in the arrivals. On the other hand, suppose that on Monday morning, a job arrives at the start of the shift, and then three more jobs arrive within the next 3 hours. Then no jobs arrive on Tuesday. Next, on Wednesday, four jobs arrive within the first 2 hours of the shift. In this scenario, there is a lot more variability in arrival times. This intuitive notion of variability can be made into a precise measure by using a concept from statistics. This concept involves the standard deviation of the times between arrivals and is explained in Appendix D (see the enclosed CD).

The second type of variability that impacts Flow Time at a resource is variability in the time that it takes for the resource to work on each job—this includes setup time plus the time to work on all the work pieces in the job. Again, let me give you an intuitive notion of this variability. Suppose that at a CNC lathe each job requires a setup time of approximately half an hour, and then it takes about an hour and a half to machine all the pieces in the job, for a total of about 2 hours per job, give or take a few minutes. Here there is very little variability in the job times. On the other hand, suppose that one job takes a total of 5 hours for setup plus machining, the next job takes only 1 hour, the next one takes 9 hours, and so on. In this scenario there is a lot of variability in the job times. Again, a precise way to measure this is given in Appendix D (see the enclosed CD).

Now I continue with explaining the impact of these two types of variability, namely arrival time variability and job time variability. For a given work center, the values of both these variability measures are squared, an important point that I will return to in the following section. These squared values are added together and divided by two—this gives the average of the variability values, which I will call *AV* for average variability. Also, let *TJ* be the average time for a job—as before, this includes setup time plus the time to work on all the work pieces in the job. All this is leading up to calculating the waiting time of a job arriving at this work center. I'll call this *QT* for queue time—this is the average time the job waits in queue until the work center has processed all the other jobs that were ahead of it.

Using *AV* and *TJ*, along with the value of *M* already explained, I can give you a very simple formula for this waiting time:

$$QT = AV \times M \times TJ$$

You can now easily calculate the Flow Time for a job visiting this resource. It is simply the average queue time plus the average time to complete the job. To summarize:

$$Flow\ time = (AV \times M \times TJ) + TJ$$

THREE-PRONGED STRATEGY TO REDUCE FLOW TIME

Inspecting this simple formula immediately gives you key insights from system dynamics. Note that this Flow Time is the amount that the visit to this resource contributes to the MCT for a job. From the formula you see clearly there are three items that magnify the Flow Time, namely *AV*, *M*, and *TJ*, so in order to reduce this Flow Time, and thereby also reduce the MCT for jobs, you need to follow the advice in the following sections.

Reduce *AV*, the Average Variability

This involves variability in both job arrivals and job times. Note that the value of *AV* involves squaring these two variabilities. Although the detailed formula is in the Appendix, you can still appreciate the point that squaring a value means that variabilities are magnified in the formula for *AV*. Conversely, even small reductions in variability are worth pursuing as they can have a substantial effect on reducing MCT. So how can you reduce variability? You need to reduce variability in both job arrivals and job times. Clearly you should target any variability that is dysfunctional variability as described in Chapter 1. Even if some of the variability in job arrivals and job times appears to be strategic variability—that is, it arises as part of your strategy to provide high variety or custom products—there can still be unnecessary variability introduced by your own organization, as the following examples show. Many times the people involved may not even realize the problems that are being created, and some investigation can help to change their mind-set and eliminate the unneeded variability. The following tips can help you in this effort.

Practical Strategies for Reducing Variability in Arrivals

The following are tips to reduce variability in job arrivals.

- Is your marketing department creating campaigns and incentives that result in big surges of orders? Perhaps these campaigns are hurting your business more than they are helping. Can the customer incentives be rethought to create a more even job flow?
- Are your salespeople gathering orders during the week while they are traveling and sending them into the office at the end of the week? With modern technology, they can e-mail or fax orders in daily, regardless of where they are.
- Are the planning or scheduling staff holding onto jobs and releasing them to the shop in batches such as once a week? Transition to daily releases, or even to releasing jobs as soon as they are processed in the office.
- Do your material handlers wait for a large load to be built up before moving it? Educate them on the importance of keeping jobs moving; they should try to move jobs as soon as they are ready, even if they are partial loads.
- Is the arrival variability a result of issues in prior operations? For example, is there an upstream machine that works very fast but also breaks down often? (When it is working it produces a lot of parts, but then no parts arrive for a while when it is down.) As another example, does an upstream operation process parts in big batches? In this case too, no parts arrive for a while, then a big batch arrives all at once.
- Use the preceding examples to brainstorm with your employees on other sources of arrival variability and how to eliminate it by use of novel procedures or simply via mind-set changes.

Practical Strategies for Reducing Variability in Job Times

Following are tips to reduce variability in job times:

- Standardize changeover procedures so that setup times are predictable.

- Similarly, standardize work procedures so that operation times are predictable.
- Plan your batch sizes so that the sum of setup and total run time remains approximately the same across jobs.
- Reduce the occurrence of rework.
- Reduce unplanned equipment downtimes by investing in preventive maintenance.
- Reduce unplanned worker absenteeism.
- Separate jobs with complex requirements from those with simple requirements (through FTMS and organizing into QRM Cells).

Reduce *M,* the Magnifying Effect of Utilization

This requires reducing resource utilization, or put differently, increasing the amount of spare capacity. This in turn implies changing planning policies so that resources are not loaded up beyond 85%. Of course this will require a shift in management mind-set to support such policies. As a result of these new planning policies, there may be some areas that are now flagged as being too highly loaded (i.e., above 85%). When such a critical resource area is detected, look for ways to increase capacity. Here are several practical strategies to do this.

Management needs to invest in creating spare capacity on critical resources. However, this does not always mean buying machines or adding people. Following are **practical ideas to reduce utilization and create spare capacity** in any area that is too highly loaded:

- Investigate opportunities to reduce setup times in this area. This does not imply large investments. Often, simple procedural improvements, investments in inexpensive fixturing, or even just creating operator awareness, can make enough of a difference.
- Invest in ways to reduce operation times. Again, small investments in efforts such as optimizing NC programs or exploring the use of improved tooling can be sufficient to add a significant slice of spare capacity.
- Can rework or scrap be reduced? This will also generate spare capacity.
- Do many of the jobs going through this resource belong to parts that are being made to stock? If so, can some of those parts be made to order once MCT has been reduced? If not, then at the very least can the quantity being made to stock be reduced since MCT will be shorter and less safety stock will be needed? (Think of it this way:

Every time you make a part that goes into a warehouse, you are steal-
ing capacity from a customer who needs it now!)

- Is there substantial machine downtime in this area? If so, invest in
preventive maintenance.
- Is there significant employee absenteeism in this area, and can that
be targeted for reduction?
- If the preceding ideas still do not provide enough spare capacity
then consider staffing the area with more people and/or adding
more equipment.

I want to add three critical notes to bolster the impact of the preceding strategies.

- Management may balk at the investments required to achieve
these improvements. However, as I pointed out earlier, even small
increases in spare capacity provide big returns in terms of Flow Time
reduction, as shown in Figure 3.2. As I also explained earlier, Flow
Time through resources often accounts for a significant portion of
your overall MCT, so reducing Flow Time has a substantial impact
on MCT. In turn, reducing MCT results in numerous financial and
organizational benefits as you have already seen—benefits that could
far exceed the investments in capacity. I will give a concrete financial
example of this in the case study at the end of this chapter.
- Supervisors and managers should realize that idle time isn't really
"idle"! When people don't have actual jobs to work on, there are
a number of other useful tasks they can perform. There is a huge
emphasis today on employees engaging in continuous improvement.
How can they spend time on brainstorming and coming up with
improvement ideas if they are always busy with their regular jobs?
Another important area to support QRM efforts, as I have emphasized, is cross-training. Again, if employees are always busy, when
will they have time to engage in cross-training? I have also discussed
the importance of setup reduction; to find ways to improve setups,
employees need to observe and analyze typical setups and then
brainstorm ways to reduce the setup time. All these activities require
time away from regularly scheduled jobs. Without spare capacity,
your employees will never have time to engage in these improvement activities. Conversely, when you have spare capacity, then during periods when there are no regular jobs to work on, employees

can spend time on these improvements. In fact, I recommend that cell teams should maintain a prioritized list of improvements that need to be made. Then, when an idle period occurs, instead of being unprepared the team can immediately pick one of the items from this list and work on it. When viewed this way, management can see that idle time is actually valuable—it is an investment in improved performance in the future—and not a waste of resources as traditional management would view it.

- A final point must be made to ensure success of these efforts. If spare capacity is indeed generated using one or more of these initiatives, then management must avoid the temptation to fill up this capacity with more jobs, or you will be back to where you started with long MCTs and all the resulting problems!

Reduce *TJ*, the Time per Job

The biggest culprit here is the fact that traditional cost-based thinking makes you run large batch sizes. If you were to cut a batch size in half, that would clearly have a big impact on the total job time. However, smaller batches also mean more setups, which eat up capacity and counter efforts to create spare capacity. So this issue is more complex than it appears at first, and I will spend more time on it in the next section of this chapter. Still, many of the ideas in the preceding section can be applied here as well, such as reducing setup time, operation time, and scrap and rework.

Combined Impact of Strategies to Reduce Flow Time

The combined impact of all these efforts is shown in Figure 3.3. There are many insights to be obtained from the graphs in that figure. First, the graphs help to summarize the lessons in the preceding sections. Let's start at the point *A* where you have a resource utilized at 90% and it also has high variability. For this example, let's say that at this point the Flow Time for jobs through this resource is 9 days. If you can reduce the utilization of this resource (moving to point *B* on the curve), that brings its Flow Time down to 6 days. Now, if you also reduce variability using the ideas in the "Reduce *AV*, the Average Variability" section, you move to point *C* on the lower curve, and that brings the Flow Time down further to 3 days. Thus, the combination of improvements—motivated by system dynamics insights—has reduced Flow Time by 67%. (The point *TJ* on the Y-axis is

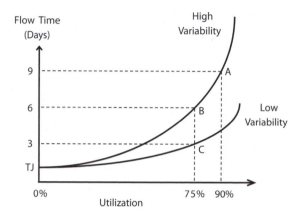

FIGURE 3.3
Combined impact of utilization and variability on Flow Time of jobs.

the average time that the resource needs to complete a job [just the setup and run time]. If the resource were idle most of the time [utilization of almost 0%] then an arriving job would have no waiting time at all, and its Flow Time would simply be the time it took to work on it. This explains why both the curves start at *TJ* when the utilization is 0%.)

Another insight is that if your business is such that high variability (in job arrivals, or job times, or both) is a given, then in order to achieve short Flow Times at resources you will need to invest in more spare capacity than in a business where variability is low, as illustrated in Figure 3.4. In that figure, point *E* is an example of a resource with low variability that

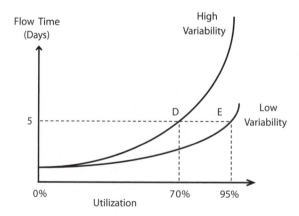

FIGURE 3.4
Businesses with higher variability need to invest in more spare capacity to keep Flow Times low.

has a Flow Time of 5 days. In a situation with higher variability, that same resource might have to operate at a utilization of 70% to achieve the 5-day Flow Time (see point *D*). So how do you know whether you need a little spare capacity or a lot? As you can see from the preceding discussion, this depends on the operating parameters for your business, and in Appendix D (on the enclosed CD) I give you more details on how to make some quick calculations to assist you with this decision.

Time-Based Approach to Batch Sizing

Since most manufacturing operations require setups—some of which may take an hour or more—it is normal practice to make parts in large batches. Indeed, most cost-based metrics reinforce this practice. Let me revisit another belief from the QRM quiz: In order to reduce our lead times, we have to improve our efficiencies (**Traditional Belief #3**).

As I mentioned in Chapter 1, belief in this principle actually results in long lead times. But this seems surprising; after all, what could be wrong with being more efficient? The answer lies in the observation that it is not the concept of efficiency that is bad, but rather, it is the measure of efficiency used by management that results in dysfunctional behavior. Most efficiency measures look something like this (for a given department and for a given period of time):

$$\text{Efficiency} = \frac{\text{Total Standard Hours of Production}}{\text{Total Hours Paid}}$$

For a given time period, such as a month, in the numerator you have the sum of the standard hours for all the parts produced by this department, and in the denominator you have the total of all the hours worked by all the people in that department. Now it is obvious that during a setup, no parts are being produced. So this measure always looks better if you engage in fewer setups and make more parts with each setup (see Figure 3.5).

The traditional belief reinforces production in large batches. But why is this bad? You might argue that if setups are being saved, this is a better (more efficient) use of your capacity, so what's wrong with that? The answer requires understanding some trade-offs with a little more help from system dynamics.

The first step toward this understanding is to look at the time that it takes to process a large batch. When there are 100 pieces in a batch,

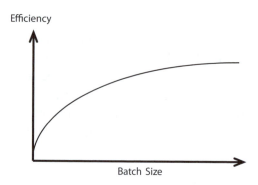

FIGURE 3.5
Traditional efficiency measures encourage production in large batches.

each operation step for that batch takes a hundred times the time for one piece. Obviously this greatly increases the time it takes for the batch to flow through your factory. But there is another important effect: it also increases the time for other jobs to get through your factory. To see this, let me bring in a few more examples from our daily lives:

- It is the day before Thanksgiving and you realize you forgot two critical items that you need for your family's Thanksgiving dinner. On your way home from work you stop at the local supermarket. You quickly grab the two items and proceed to the checkout area, only to find that the "fast checkout" lane is closed that day. You get stuck in a line behind two families that have huge carts full of groceries for their Thanksgiving dinners. So even though you have only two items to buy, you end up taking more than 20 minutes to check out. In manufacturing terms, even though you have a small batch, you get stuck behind two large batches and end up with a large Flow Time.
- You are driving cross-country on an interstate highway and have a deadline to meet, but need to make a quick stop for lunch. You see the sign for a fast-food chain and take the exit to the restaurant. Normally you should be able to get in and out of this place in a matter of minutes. But just before you get to the fast-food restaurant, a school bus pulls up and 40 kids run into the restaurant and line up at the counter. There is no way that you are going to get your lunch in a matter of minutes. (You would probably get back in your car and back on the interstate, and look for the next fast-food stop!) Once again, in manufacturing terms, as long as the fast-food restaurant

was serving small groups of customers (small batches), people got served in a matter of minutes. But when a big batch arrived, then customers behind the big batch had to wait much longer.

These examples from everyday life reinforce the point that big batches lead to long waiting times. At the same time though, in the manufacturing context where setups are involved, it is also true that larger batches help by reducing the unproductive time spent in setups. So what is the right approach, small batches or large batches? The answer lies in between: There is a trade-off involved and you need to understand this further in order to make better decisions that will help in reducing Flow Time. You may have seen a batch size trade-off analysis using the Economic Order Quantity (EOQ) calculation. The approach here is quite different. While the EOQ analysis uses *cost* as its basis, my approach, in keeping with QRM philosophy, uses *time* as its basis. I point out the many pitfalls of the traditional EOQ analysis in the "System Dynamics Compared with MRP, EOQ, and Other Traditional Approaches" section later in this chapter.

The technical details of the batch size trade-off can be studied using mathematics from system dynamics, but here I will illustrate the main points using a graph. Figure 3.6 shows the impact of batch sizes on Flow Time. Start at the point Z on the right side of the graph. Here very large batch sizes are being used, and as explained in the preceding examples, Flow Times are long for two reasons: each batch takes a long time to get through each operation, and batches wait for long times behind other big batches that are occupying the resources they need. Next, as you move toward the center of the graph, the batch sizes become smaller, and jobs start moving through the factory faster, so Flow Times go down. However, these smaller batches require more setups. As more and more time is used

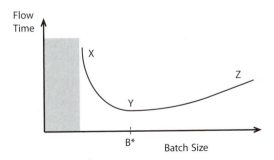

FIGURE 3.6
System dynamics shows the true impact of batch size on Flow Time.

in setups, the resources in the factory become more highly utilized. Now you know from earlier in this chapter that as resources become busier, the queue times at these resources increase. So this queue time gets larger and larger, and after a certain point, namely point Y, the total Flow Time starts to increase. This explains why the graph starts to go back up as you move farther left toward point X. You get to the point (demarcated by the "wall" in the graph) where the batch size is so small that you are spending almost all your time in setups and you have no capacity left to make products, so jobs take a very long time to get through the factory and the Flow Time increases substantially.

With the insights from Figure 3.6, I can now state the QRM principle that must replace **Traditional Belief #3.** While the traditional management belief aims at improving efficiencies, the QRM approach is the following: make MCT reduction the main performance measure. De-emphasize or eliminate other measures such as utilization and efficiency (**QRM Principle #3**).

Since Flow Times at all the resources contribute to MCT, this principle also implies that you need to reduce these Flow Times. So while the traditional approach encourages production in large batches (as seen from Figure 3.5), QRM drives your enterprise to use the batch size indicated by B^* in Figure 3.6. This is the batch size that leads to the shortest Flow Time. Now this batch size may require more setups than the traditional approach, so let me argue why your enterprise should strive for this batch size. The graph in Figure 3.6 is based on a system dynamics analysis with a fixed number of resources (machines and people), and only the batch size is varied. Since the resources are fixed, the cost of these resources remains constant. However, from Chapter 1 you know that there are numerous enterprise-wide costs associated with a long MCT. Hence those costs are greater for longer Flow Times. Thus the lowest value of these other costs will be obtained at the batch size marked B^*. Since the resource costs are fixed for this whole analysis, the total system costs will also be minimized at this point. In addition, with the shortest Flow Times you also obtain high quality and customer satisfaction due to quick response.

Thus the QRM approach encourages an enterprise to strive toward using batch sizes that minimize Flow Times. So how do you find these batch sizes for your operation? I will give you several ways to do this; two involve rules of thumb and are simple to pursue initially, one involves more analysis of your data, and one is more complex and involves use of dynamic modeling software.

The first rule of thumb is one that I have arrived at after two decades of analyzing manufacturing enterprises: batch sizes in use at most companies are invariably too large. The reason for this is that they were derived using cost-based rules that do not incorporate any system dynamics, thereby greatly underestimating the dysfunctional impact of these large batches. What this means is that even without further analysis, you can start experimenting with smaller batch sizes and expect to see the improvements in terms of Flow Time almost immediately. Two caveats are in order here before you charge down this path: first, if any of your products go through a resource (or resources) that is a severe bottleneck, don't reduce the batch sizes on those—see the next few paragraphs for additional ideas; and second, reduce the batch sizes in small steps, rather than making drastic reductions—for example, try 15% to 20% reductions at a time. As you do this, either you will see reductions in work-in-process and Flow Times, in which case you can repeat the process with another small reduction in batch sizes, or you will observe that a certain resource is starting to become a bottleneck. In that case, you should proceed with the advice at the end of this section about what to do. The advantage of this empirical approach is that you can proceed carefully but also you don't need a lot of analysis ahead of time so you can implement it quickly.

The second rule of thumb involves a formula, albeit a simple one, and is explained in Appendix D (see the enclosed CD). A third approach requires analysis of specific data for the resource and the details are also included in Appendix D. A final alternative requires use of more complex dynamic modeling software for companies that have expertise in using these tools. Recommendations for how to use these methods to support your QRM program are also in Appendix D. For many companies, the use of QRM Cells along with the first three approaches should be sufficient to provide substantial reductions in MCT without having to resort to using the more complex software tools.

In fact this brings up an important point about the order in which you should follow the QRM principles. It is essential that you create the right organizational structure first, using the concept of FTMS and organizing into QRM Cells. Don't start by trying to reduce batch sizes within the existing organization structure. Of course you don't have to change your entire shop floor before you reduce batch sizes—you can begin with one or more FTMSs and corresponding QRM Cells, and then start reducing the batch sizes for the associated products. Also, with cells in place it is much easier for the cell teams to be aware of their bottlenecks and thus apply the rules of thumb appropriately.

As batch sizes are reduced, if cells start to experience bottlenecks, then they should alleviate those bottlenecks using the ideas in the "Reduce M, the Magnifying Effect of Utilization" section earlier in this chapter. One of those ideas involves setup reduction and it is useful to spend a little time on this particular idea. There is a lot of emphasis on setup reduction these days, so this is not a novel idea at all. However, system dynamics enables managers to get new insights into the value of setup reduction—insights that might motivate them to pursue it with more vigor.

Setup Reduction—Insights from System Dynamics

Figure 3.7 uses system dynamics analysis to demonstrate the impact of setup reduction on the Flow Time at a resource. The upper graph in this figure, labeled "Before," is a portion of the U-shaped curve that we saw in Figure 3.6, and it displays the impact of batch size on Flow Time at a resource. On the horizontal axis, which represents batch size, the point BB (for "Batch size Before") represents the batch size in use in a cell before any setup improvements are made. At this time the Flow Time through the resource has the value FTB (for "Flow Time Before") as shown in the figure. Now by successively reducing the batch size, the cell team can attempt to find the point BB* that reduces the Flow Time through this resource to FTB*, which is the lowest value that can be achieved as it is the lowest point on the U-shaped curve.

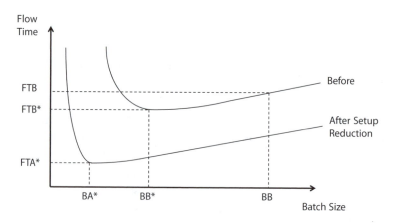

FIGURE 3.7

Combined impact of setup reduction and batch size on Flow Time.

Now let's see what happens if the team can reduce the setup time on this resource by 50%. System dynamics analysis shows that the U-shaped curve moves down and to the left, as shown by the curve marked "After Setup Reduction" in Figure 3.7. Although the details derive from mathematical equations, intuitively this shift can be easily explained. Since for any batch size that is being used, reducing setup time would invariably reduce Flow Time, you can see that for each batch size the Flow Time should be lower; i.e., the curve should move downward in general. Next, with a 50% setup reduction in place, it should be possible to run smaller batch sizes before this resource becomes a serious bottleneck. Hence the curve should move to the left. These two arguments explain the position of the new U-shaped curve.

The new curve illustrates the huge opportunity that is now available. The cell team can reduce batch sizes all the way down to BA* (for Batch size After), at which point the Flow Time value will be reduced to FTA* (Flow Time After). When you compare it to the initial value FTB, the value FTA* represents about an 80% reduction of Flow Time. Thus the system dynamics analysis helps to illustrate the huge impact of setup reduction combined with batch size reduction.

The value of this strategy is typically underestimated by management, or else it is misunderstood. Using traditional thinking, management sees setup reduction as a way of reducing setup costs and at the same time creating more capacity so more parts can be produced at the resource. But in fact you may not reduce traditional setup costs. Consider a simple calculation. Suppose you reduce the setup time on a machine by 50%. Then let's say you cut your batch sizes on that machine by 50% as well. Since you will be setting up twice as often, but the setup time has been halved, the total time you spend in setups will be the same as before, so your traditional setup costs remain the same. Thus the traditional cost analysis would show no benefit of this strategy. But in actual fact, as Figure 3.7 shows, your MCT will be reduced substantially and you will get the numerous benefits of reduced company-wide costs, improved responsiveness, and so on, as I have discussed many times in this book.

Setup reduction is an important part of the strategy for Flow Time reduction and Figure 3.7 provides a vivid illustration of this, but setup reduction is only one of many techniques that can be used. The key point is that in order to enable batch size reduction, you will need to add capacity at a few resources, and you should use the ideas in the "Reduce *M*, the Magnifying Effect of Utilization" section presented earlier in this chapter.

Reexamining Organizational Policies to Support Batch Size Reduction

To support the batch size reduction efforts, you also need to reexamine policies in other parts of your organization, particularly in three areas: materials management, sales, and cost accounting, as follows.

- In terms of materials management policies, for parts that are being made to stock consider making smaller quantities. This will reinforce a downward spiral of Flow Times as follows. The smaller batches will result in shorter Flow Times so that lower values of lead time can be used in planning and MRP calculations. The lower lead times will mean that less safety stock is needed since replenishment can be accomplished more quickly. Less safety stock will then mean that where the forecast was too high, fewer parts will now be made for these cases. This also means that less capacity will be wasted on incorrect parts that sit in stock. In turn, the availability of more capacity will mean that smaller batches can be run. And so on. Now remember that Flow Times add to the MCT value, and also time spent in stock adds to your MCT. Hence the combination of shorter Flow Times and less stock will result in lower MCT for your organization.

- In terms of sales policies, for parts that are being made for specific customers in large batches, ask why this is necessary. Chances are that those customers need only a few parts every day or every week, but they have placed a large order because of incentives provided by your sales organization. Traditionally we assume that making a larger batch will provide a higher profit margin due to less setup time, so we encourage salespeople to land larger orders. However, now you see that the resulting dysfunctional effects can quickly eat up these profits and cause havoc to your enterprise. So here too, explore the opportunity for making smaller batches for your customers, provided that the shipping costs don't become prohibitive. You can still give them quantity discounts based on total quantity ordered over a period such as a year, but make and deliver the parts in smaller batches. In most cases the customers will be pleased by your efforts because it will mean that they, too, can carry less inventory.

- In terms of costing policies, you need to overcome one major obstacle: traditional costing methods will show that the smaller batch sizes used for parts going through a QRM Cell will increase the standard cost of those parts, and so management may not be happy with the reports from the costing system. There are two ways to alleviate this problem, and they can be used in conjunction with each other to reinforce their effect. The first is that if you reduce setup times for the operations in the cell, the smaller batch sizes may not increase the standard costs, or at least, not as much. For example, if the setup times are reduced by 50%, then reducing batch sizes by 50% results in exactly the same standard cost as before. The second is to reexamine the overhead allocated to the parts going through the cell. Following the QRM arguments made throughout this book, the shorter MCT for these parts means that overhead costs related to these parts should be much lower. I will have more to say about this strategy in Chapter 5, but a simple numerical example will help to make my point here. Let's say the standard cost of a part is $1,000, made up as follows: $400 for material, $100 for labor, and $500 for overhead. (This is similar to the breakdown shown in Chapter 1, Figure 1.4.) Suppose the batch size for this part is cut in half so that for a given annual quantity twice as many setups are required, and suppose for this calculation that the setup times are not reduced. Now some of the labor time is for setups and some is for run time, so the labor cost won't double, but let's say it goes up by $50 per piece. If the overhead costs related to this part go down by just 10%, that would reduce overhead by $50 and exactly offset the labor cost increase. In actual fact, QRM company experiences have been much better—overheads have gone down by 25% to 50% for parts made in QRM Cells. Combining the two arguments here (setup time reduction and overhead allocation reduction), you see that with the right support from management, you can indeed find a way to support the smaller batch sizes and still look good with the traditional cost measures.

Even reducing a few of the largest batch sizes can have a substantial impact. The following data is based on a system dynamics analysis of a manufacturing facility. A particular cell made 40 jobs a month, each with a batch size of around 5 pieces per order, plus it made 2 jobs a month where the customers needed 110 pieces in each order. I was suspicious about the impact of these large batch sizes (110) on the operation of the cell when most of the other jobs in the cell had a batch size of 5. The setup times on the jobs were around two hours, with a 15-minute run time per piece, so management seemed happy to run the large jobs.

On the other hand, a simple system dynamics analysis showed that the cell could actually run all the orders with a batch size of 5 and the resulting reduction of Flow Time through the cell would be dramatic. With the current operation, the Flow Time for the small jobs was 33 hours and for the large jobs it was 67 hours. Now what if each of the monthly orders of 110 pieces for the two customers were to be broken down into a daily demand? Assuming 20 working days in a month, this would bring the job size down to a daily quantity of around 5 pieces, right in line with the other batch sizes. Next, the analysis showed that if all the jobs were done in batch sizes of 5, even though this would mean that many more setups would need to be done every month for the orders of 110 pieces, the Flow Time for all jobs would be reduced to 11 hours. In other words, the cell would achieve a 67% reduction in Flow Time for the small jobs and over 80% reduction for the large jobs! This example illustrates the dysfunctional impact that even a few large batch sizes can have on your whole operation. Not only did the large jobs have long Flow Times, but these two large customer orders also created long Flow Times for the small orders.

QRM Approach to Transfer Batching

There is one other batch-sizing method used in an attempt to reduce Flow Times, and it is called transfer batching (sometimes also called one-piece flow, particularly in the context of Lean Manufacturing). The idea here is that when a batch of parts needs operations at several different resources, instead of waiting for the whole batch to be finished at a resource before moving it, you move each piece from one resource to the next as soon as it is completed (hence the "one-piece flow" name). If operations are not near each other, this might involve too much material handling, but you can still use the idea by transferring smaller batches of parts; e.g., if the batch size is 100, you could transfer 20 pieces at a time—here you would say the transfer batch size is 20, and hence the "transfer batch" name.

While transfer batching might well help to reduce Flow Time and is always worth considering, in the QRM context several other points should also be taken into account before adopting this strategy. In fact, I have visited many companies whose management is perplexed because even though they have implemented one-piece flow they still have very long Flow Times. The following points will give you insight into this issue:

- As seen from the preceding example where the two big customer orders were reduced in size, system dynamics analysis shows that in general, reduction of the overall batch size has a much greater effect than implementing transfer batching. It may of course be necessary to combine setup reduction or other capacity-increasing techniques along with the batch size reduction, as explained already. In any case, given the magnitude of Flow Time reductions possible, these strategies should take precedence over implementing transfer batching.
- With QRM Cells in place, cell teams can be educated in transfer batching and encouraged to use it within their cell if they feel it would be helpful. Since the teams have ownership of the operation within each cell, they can decide when transfer batching is best used—for example, only for certain parts or certain flow patterns within the cell. Again, the first priority for the teams should be reduction of overall batch size, along with setup reduction or other supporting improvements if needed, and the transfer batching should come in only after those efforts are in place.
- In terms of transferring parts between cells, in QRM this is accomplished using the material control strategy called POLCA, which I will describe in the next chapter. Here too, the transfer batching strategy (and transfer batch size if applicable) will depend on decisions related to how POLCA is implemented.

The preceding comments drive home the point that transfer batching should not be your initial strategy, but should be applied in the context of the broader QRM strategies being used in your organization. This discussion also helps to explain why those companies mentioned did not find much benefit from transfer batching—they had not implemented the more fundamental strategies such as reorganizing into cells and releasing small overall batches, and so the transfer batching had little impact on their operation.

SYSTEM DYNAMICS COMPARED WITH MRP, EOQ, AND OTHER TRADITIONAL APPROACHES

This chapter has highlighted the importance of system dynamics in reducing Flow Times. If you already have other planning systems in place, you might be wondering, "Can I use those systems instead and will they give me some of the same insights?" Unfortunately, the answer is "No!"—because the majority of traditional planning approaches do not incorporate system dynamics in their analysis. I will explain this for three commonly used approaches to planning and batch sizing.

The first and probably most widespread approach today involves the use of MRP or ERP systems. The acronym MRP derives from the earliest of these systems where it stood for Material Requirements Planning. When the functionality of these systems was expanded, they were named MRP II systems and the acronym then stood for Manufacturing Resource Planning. Today even more business functions have been added and the new systems are called Enterprise Resource Planning or ERP systems. For the purpose of this discussion though, you should know that the core production planning logic used in ERP and MRP II systems remains the same as in the original MRP approach, so the comments here apply equally to MRP, MRP II, and ERP systems, and henceforth I shall just use the original term MRP in this explanation. To explain why MRP systems don't provide the right insights to support Flow Time reduction, I need to tell you about a few features in their design:

- These systems use static models in their calculations. What this means is that the workload for a resource, for a given period, is obtained by adding up all the work assigned to that resource during that period. However, this workload number is not incorporated into any system dynamics analysis.
- Lead time for each operation is provided by the planners as an input to the system. Hence, the system doesn't tell you the impact of decisions on lead times because you tell it what you think the lead time will be. (I use "lead time" here because that is the term used in the MRP system, but you can interpret this as Flow Time for this discussion.)
- There is no change to the given lead times based on capacity calculations. As you saw clearly in Figure 3.1, your lead times can vary significantly with capacity utilization, particularly as you approach high utilizations.
- As mentioned in the first item, in these systems the workload for each resource is calculated for each time period (e.g., day or week). However, the period during which each job will arrive at the resource is based on the lead time in the MRP system. As just explained, lead

times can change significantly (be much shorter or much longer) depending on the utilization of upstream resources. Thus jobs can arrive at resources earlier or later than planned. This means the time-phased capacity calculation is not valid. For instance, it often happens that in a period that the system predicts a very high workload in an area, few jobs actually arrive. On the other hand, a week later when the system predicted that there would not be much work (and the supervisor authorized vacations for several people!) a whole bunch of jobs arrive.

Thus you see that MRP systems can't really support Flow Time reduction because there are several deficiencies in the way they are designed. In other words, MRP systems won't provide the right insights that will help management make decisions that will reduce Flow Time.

A second approach to capacity planning is used by companies that have their own "home-grown" systems, which typically use spreadsheets to predict the capacity usage on key resources. Since these spreadsheet calculations are also based on static calculations, they suffer from similar drawbacks as the MRP systems just described. So these systems too don't predict how various decisions would affect Flow Times and MCT.

Third, many companies use Economic Order Quantity (EOQ) models to set their batch sizes. This approach is often used along with one of the other approaches listed. For a given product, the EOQ model attempts to trade off the setup cost with the inventory holding cost, to arrive at the "optimum" batch size that minimizes the total of these two costs for that product. The discussion and the figures in this chapter help to point out that the EOQ approach has many errors and misses several significant issues that are important for QRM:

- You saw in Figure 3.6 that batch size has a significant impact on Flow Time, which then impacts MCT. Chapter 1 showed the huge impact of MCT on cost. The EOQ model does not take into account the impact of batch size on MCT, nor does it account for the impact of MCT on cost.
- The EOQ value is calculated independently for each product. In other words, it is assumed that the EOQ for one product has no affect on another product. However, the example in the preceding section showed how the jobs made in batches of 110 pieces had a huge impact on the Flow Time of other jobs in the cell. In other words, EOQ could

lead you to set batch sizes for one product that really hurt your delivery of other products.

- The EOQ model does not place any value on responsiveness. Chapters 1 and 2 showed you the many ways that being responsive can have a positive impact on your business and also lower your costs.

This discussion has highlighted some key ways in which MRP systems, spreadsheet-based planning, and EOQ models can misguide you in your MCT reduction efforts. The two key reasons behind this are that they do not include system dynamics in their calculations, and they do not account for the cost of long MCT, or conversely, the value of responsiveness. In fact, since in traditional manufacturing and business education managers are not taught about these basic principles and insights derived from system dynamics, they are not aware of the drawbacks of the traditional decision-making tools in use at their companies. The following real-world case study—involving some very large sums of money—helps drive home this point.

WHY COMPANIES MISTAKENLY INVEST IN WAREHOUSES INSTEAD OF MACHINES

Whenever I talk about the need for spare capacity, I hear loud protests from managers about how this will increase the cost of their operations. A real-world example helps to show how misdirected this reasoning can be—companies end up buying warehouses instead of machines!

A large corporation had a division that made parts for the aerospace industry and had lead times of 8 to 10 weeks for those parts. Since those parts were primarily made for the spares market, they had to be available in stock to be shipped at short notice. This division made over 5,000 different part types, and stocked about ten pieces of each on average. As these parts were made with a high-tech alloy and involved sophisticated machining, the cost of each piece was over $1,000. A simple multiplication of these three numbers shows us that this division was carrying over $50 million worth of finished goods inventories in its many warehouses.

When I investigated the operations at the division, three things became clear to me:

- Because of the large number of products and their different machining requirements, as well as the unpredictability of spare parts demand, there was high variability in their operations.
- Due to corporate metrics that emphasized asset utilization, most of the machines were loaded up with jobs so that they ran as much of the time as possible (high utilization).
- Due to the way manufacturing management was measured (i.e., efficiency measures), there was a built-in incentive to run large batch sizes.

The cumulative impact of these three effects was that their parts had very long lead times, which necessitated the large finished-goods stock.

A rough analysis of their operations showed that if management invested in four CNC machines to provide capacity in a few critical areas, along with the staff needed to run these machines for two shifts a day, there would be enough additional capacity to cut the batch sizes significantly while still leaving some spare capacity. The net result of these recommendations would be to reduce the lead time by 70%, to under 3 weeks. With the large reduction in lead time, much less safety stock would need to be carried for each item and the inventory could also be reduced by around 70%. However, I was unable to get the division's management to implement the recommendations! Why?

Senior management at this division was evaluated at the corporate level by the utilization and efficiency measures that I mentioned. The addition of machines and creation of spare capacity would lower their utilization numbers, the smaller batch sizes would lower their efficiency numbers, and these smaller batches would also raise their standard costs for products. In other words they would look bad, bad, and bad!

Let's look at some numbers though. Four CNC machines would have cost them a onetime investment of around $3 million including installation and training. Two shifts of four operators each (total of eight more operators) would have cost them around a million dollars a year, including benefits and other direct costs. On the plus side, since finished goods would be reduced by 70%, they would realize a reduction of $35 million in inventory. Now you can choose whatever cost-benefit analysis method you want, but to me, investing $3 million once plus $1 million annually to liberate $35 million in assets, is a no-brainer! Here's a simple way to think about it. After the implementation is completed and you have bled down the excess inventory, you have $32 million in cash that you didn't have before ($35 million less the $3 million that you forked out for the machines). Yes, you are spending a million dollars a year more than you were. But what is the opportunity cost of pumping $32 million back into your business? Most companies work with opportunity costs in the double digits (as a percentage)—management looks for projects that can return 20% or even much higher on any investment that they make. Even with a modest opportunity cost of 15%, the $32 million is worth around $5 million a year—far more than the $1 million being paid in additional salaries.

This is just part of the story though. I haven't even included all the warehouse operating and management costs that would be eliminated. And there are even bigger savings and opportunities to take into account. With shorter lead times, the division would also realize overhead reductions in other parts of its operations as discussed in Chapter 1. In addition, it would realize higher quality, an improved ability to respond quickly to demand changes, increased customer satisfaction, and many other benefits already discussed in this book. So there would have been an even higher long-term return than my rough calculation showed.

Why did these arguments not work with the division's management? Because the division's management was not penalized for the warehouse operations—those operations were measured by the corporation's distribution side of the business. In fact, those metrics made the people in charge of the warehouse look better when they had *more* inventory.

This is where top management in companies needs to truly understand the impact of system dynamics. First, there is the smaller lesson of understanding the impact of system dynamics on the operation of each resource. Then, by putting the pieces together, there is the bigger lesson that local investments in spare capacity (which may add to cost) can result in global improvements and systemwide reductions in cost that far exceed the local investments.

In conclusion, system dynamics plays a critical role in the behavior of your manufacturing system, particularly when it comes to Flow Times and MCT. A cornerstone of QRM is to give managers and employees a basic understanding of system dynamics and some of the key trade-offs as illustrated in the graphs in this chapter. Even without going into the detailed mathematical theory behind these graphs, by simply being aware of these trade-offs managers and employees can avoid inadvertently making poor decisions that lengthen Flow Times. Instead, they can begin to ask the right questions and make more informed decisions that will support significant reduction of Flow Times and hence MCT.

4

A Unified Strategy for the Whole Enterprise

"At last! A manufacturing strategy that goes beyond just optimizing the shop floor!" I hear this enthusiastic remark often as managers and employees learn more about QRM and realize how it can be used to improve the entire organization. True, thus far I have mainly told you how to apply QRM to reorganize the shop floor and provided new ways to look at capacity planning for your factory resources. However, QRM is not just a shop floor strategy; it applies throughout your enterprise. The same time-based mind-set and principles that have been discussed thus far extend to all areas of your organization. This is one of the strengths of QRM: Instead of having different approaches for different parts of your organization, you have one unified strategy for the whole enterprise.

You will see how QRM extends beyond the shop floor to your office operations, materials-planning systems, supply chain, and even accounting. More specifically, in this chapter, I show you how to:

- Achieve quick response in your office operations such as estimating and quoting, engineering, scheduling, and order processing.
- Restructure your materials-planning system to support QRM.
- Implement POLCA, a shop floor control system for low-volume or custom-engineered products.
- Transform your purchasing operations using Time-Based Supply Management.
- Implement quick response in new-product introduction.

Chapter 5 will then give you a road map for successful implementation of QRM in your organization, including ways to adjust your accounting and cost-justification methods to support QRM.

PRINCIPLES OF QUICK RESPONSE IN OFFICE OPERATIONS

Office operations such as quoting, engineering, scheduling, and order processing tend to be neglected as a source of improvement in manufacturing companies. Yet these operations can:

- Consume more than half of your quoted lead time
- Account for over 25% of your costs
- Greatly influence your order capture rate
- Impact your overall market share

The reason for this large impact is that office operations impact both your overhead costs as well as your selling, general, and administrative (SG&A) expenses. Office operations can also impact your order capture rate and overall market share in two ways: first, if you take too long to respond to requests for quotes, you can lose orders right off the bat; and second, if customers perceive long response times in both the quoting and processing of orders, they could be reluctant to give you future orders.

At the same time, management neglects the office operations as a target for improvement for several reasons. Traditionally, going back to the days of Henry Ford and other pioneers of scientific management, manufacturing companies have always focused on the shop floor for improvements. This focus is promoted by costing systems that assume that product cost is driven by direct labor and/or machine times. Furthermore, while there are usually a lot of measurements on the shop floor, there is an absence of measurement of time spent by orders or other jobs in the office, and in particular no clear measurement of how office processes contribute to overall MCT. Finally, there is a lack of appreciation by management of the multiple benefits of MCT reduction, and as a result, no significant motivation to measure and reduce the component of MCT that is due to office operations.

The Response Time Spiral in Office Operations

In fact, office lead times grow insidiously, so that they are not noticed thanks to another Response Time Spiral, this one in the office. As shown in Figure 4.1, the spiral begins with long lead times, which departments

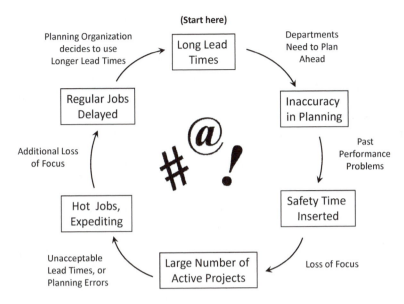

FIGURE 4.1
The Response Time Spiral in office operations.

are required to plan ahead for when they promise to complete each job. (As in preceding chapters, I use "lead time" when I just need an intuitive interpretation of this concept or for situations where this term is commonly used in industry, such as in planning and quoting. I use "MCT" when I refer to a precise metric that can be used to set goals and is specifically related to QRM efforts. Note that office operations are an important component of your overall MCT—see Chapter 1, and also Appendix A on the enclosed CD.) Since the plans cannot be perfect—and based on past performance problems—departments or planners insert safety time into each department's lead time. For example, let's say a custom-engineered order needs a few hours of design engineering. This work could be completed by an engineer in less than a day. However, since the Engineering Department has a lot of jobs to work on, the planner might allow for 5 days of lead time. The past performance problems then influence this decision further. On several occasions, the Engineering Department has been buried with warranty issues and other production emergencies that have soaked up the engineers' time. On these occasions, new orders have been held up and eventually delivered late to the customer. So the Planning Department decides to add another week of safety time to the lead time for

Engineering, just in case such events occur again. Similarly, safety time is added to other departments that the job must visit.

Because of the longer departmental lead times, each department, such as Engineering, now has a large number of active jobs in the department, which causes a loss of focus. The problem is compounded by planning errors, which means that jobs need to be expedited. Or else, the overall long lead times are found unacceptable by customers, and in order to secure an order, the sales organization agrees to a "special" shorter lead time. Again, such jobs need to be expedited. These expedited jobs (or hot jobs) take all the attention, leading to an additional loss of focus on the regular jobs, which means that those jobs take even longer to get through the department. Based on a few such occurrences, which result in late deliveries to customers, the Planning Department decides to add even more safety time to that department's lead time. And so the spiral grows and gets worse.

Why does this spiral occur? The roots of the spiral are the same as explained in Chapter 2 and summarized in Figure 2.6 there. Just as on the shop floor, the scale/cost thinking led companies to break up office tasks into small pieces, with each piece being done by the lowest skilled person that could accomplish it. You know this happens on the shop floor but may be surprised by the fact that this happens in office operations, so let me give you a few examples. Companies often have order entry departments, where clerks review orders received (by mail, fax, or the Internet) and then enter them into a computer system. The clerks don't know about product design or materials or scheduling, so they usually can't catch inconsistencies and certainly can't make any decisions; all they do is enter the data and then other staff have to review the orders. For this job, the clerks need only reading and typing skills. Another example is the Drafting Department. A design engineer will complete a design for a part and then hand it over to the Drafting Department for a person to create the detailed drawings. The idea is that this saves the valuable time of the higher paid engineer and replaces it with the less valuable time of the lower paid drafting person.

However, as I explained in detail in Chapter 2, this structure creates many functional departments with lots of handoffs to process each job. Further, the cost reduction emphasis makes these departments operate at high utilizations, causing large backlogs, long lead times, quality problems, and eventually higher (not reduced!) costs for the whole organization.

Most organizations don't realize how contorted their process has become, and in many cases don't even know that they have a problem in their office operations. A manufacturer of parts for the automotive industry asked me to help them reduce their lead time for making prototypes. Getting the prototypes to their customers on time was key in terms of landing a big contract for large numbers of those parts in the future. However this company was often weeks late in delivering the prototypes and was losing contracts because the competition's part had already been selected by then. When I started the project with them, they felt the problem was in manufacturing and sent me to look over the production process for the prototypes. I soon realized, though, that production accounted for a very small part of the total lead time—most of the time was in the office. Over the years the office process had gotten out of control: Figure 4.2 shows the lengthy flow of the process prior to release to manufacturing.

Clearly this process was extremely complex and time consuming. But the worst part of it was that no one in the organization was aware of the extent of the whole process and so no one had realized how inefficient this was! This example drives home my earlier point that companies do not measure (and hence do not know) much about their office processes, and do not even see the vast opportunities for improvement that exist in their office operations. Hence it is important that you extend your MCT metric to office operations as well. Appendix A (on the enclosed CD) provides detailed examples of how to do this.

Eliminating the Response Time Spiral in Office Operations

So how do you get rid of the Response Time Spiral in the office and reduce the office component of your overall MCT? You need to shift from cost-based thinking to time-based thinking just like we did for the shop floor. Once again, it is useful to understand that this is a significant change in mind-set; a simple example helps to drive home this point.

Figure 4.3 shows a summary of actual data obtained from observing around 100 orders flowing through the office at a company that makes small machined parts. Orders typically go through four office departments before they are released to the shop floor for production. The "elapsed time" numbers give the average time spent in each department while the "touch time" is the average amount of actual work done by people in each department (this terminology is the same as that used in Chapter 1, and the touch time is again shown in gray in Figure 4.3). The summary line on the figure says it all—it took an average of 12.6 working days to accomplish a total of less than one hour of actual work! I had been asked to

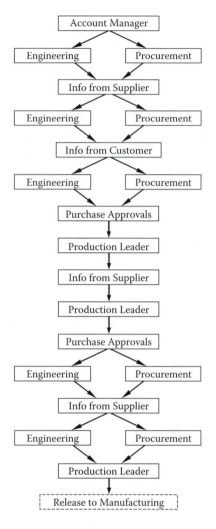

FIGURE 4.2
Process flow showing the numerous office operations performed prior to production of prototype.

help reduce lead times at this company, and as in many other situations, they told me that their office lead times were "only a couple of days" and I should focus on the shop floor. Our data analysis was an eye-opener not only for management, but also for the office employees, who realized that there was a lot of scope for improvement and thereby bought into the need for our QRM project. Again this example underscores the importance of extending the MCT metric into office operations.

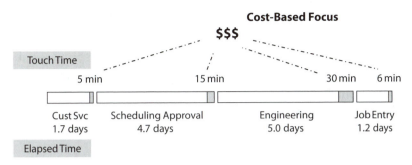

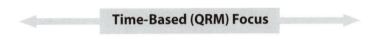

Office Component of MCT: **12.6 days** for about **1 hour** of work

FIGURE 4.3
Difference between cost-based and QRM approaches for office operations.

Continuing with this example, the cost-based approach would focus on reducing the time spent by people at each step (the gray space). In this case, the biggest opportunity would be the 30 minutes spent by an engineer, both because it represents the most time and because that is the most expensive resource in this route. So management would try to find ways to reduce the engineering time, such as buying newer CAD software to automate some of the tasks or even outsourcing some of the engineering work. But even if the engineering time were to be cut in half, to 15 minutes, the total office portion of their MCT would barely be affected at all—reducing 12.6 days by 15 minutes would not even be noticeable!

Instead, as shown in the figure, the time-based approach looks at the entire process from start to finish and finds ways to reduce this total time. To summarize the differences between the cost-based and time-based approaches, let us revisit the traditional belief discussed in Chapter 1, and its QRM counterpart:

- **Traditional Belief #1:** Everyone will have to work faster, harder, and longer hours, in order to get jobs done in less time.
- **QRM Principle #1:** Find whole new ways of completing a job, with a primary focus on minimizing MCT.

So what are these "whole new ways"? They are based on the same principles already described, namely the organizational principles in

Chapter 2 and the system dynamics concepts in Chapter 3. Once again, this serves to highlight the point that the same QRM principles extend across the whole organization. I will now illustrate the specific application of these principles to the office environment, beginning with the organizational principles.

I will apply the same four principles described in Chapter 2 to the office environment:

- Reorganize your functional departments into QRM Cells. In the office context, we call these Quick Response Office Cells, or Q-ROCs (pronounced "queue-rocks"), described further in the two following sections.
- Move from top-down control to ownership by the Q-ROCs.
- Progress from specialized, narrowly-focused employees to cross-trained team members in the Q-ROCs.
- Replace your efficiency/utilization goals with MCT reduction measured via the QRM Number for each Q-ROC.

I will go into more detail on all these in the following sections, but first, I must warn you of a potential pitfall—don't try to reorganize your whole office into cells all at once. This is often the failure of reengineering or other improvement efforts. You must start by identifying an FTMS (Focused Target Market Segment) as explained in Chapter 2, and form a Q-ROC around this FTMS; then repeat for other FTMSs. For your convenience a quick summary of FTMS is given here, but you may wish to review the detailed explanation of FTMS in Chapter 2 before proceeding.

How to Identify an FTMS in the Context of Office Operations

Begin by looking for a market segment where there is an opportunity via a quick response strategy. Here "market" can be an external or an internal customer that requires shorter response times. Examine the office-processing steps for this segment, and be sure to identify the "product" of these steps. For example, a product of office processing could be a quote to a customer, a purchase order to a supplier, or a work order released to the shop floor. For the product that you have focused on, you will probably notice that the office process is long and involved with many steps through many departments. Now ask yourself, is there a subset of this "product" that can be attacked with simpler processing steps—in other words, don't try to design for the worst-case (most complex) scenario. (These simpler steps can be obtained by restricting or reconsidering product options, as well as by rethinking how processing steps are done—I will give examples of this in the two following sections.) Next, see if this subset represents a significant enough demand that it is worth pursuing as a focus. If so, proceed to designing the Q-ROC as explained below. If not, go back to the first step and rethink the market segment or start with an entirely different market segment. Continue this process until you have arrived at a subset that appears to be worth focusing on. This is the FTMS for your office QRM project. This does not mean that you will abandon the orders or customers that require more complex steps; these will still be fulfilled the way that they are done today, using the existing processes, and then they can be the target of a future QRM project.

This process of identifying an FTMS should be conducted by a cross-functional group that includes people from marketing and sales, the office areas involved, engineering, purchasing, manufacturing, and possibly other relevant functions. The reason is that brainstorming to get a good FTMS is key to the success of your Q-ROC, and the cross-functional team will include enough expertise to think outside the box for alternatives that may be possible for restricting the various product options and rethinking processing steps. To help you with this brainstorming process, Appendix B (on the enclosed CD) provides a number of pointers on how to arrive at a good FTMS.

In order to help you grasp the main idea without having to read Appendix B, here are some examples of criteria used to arrive at an FTMS. You can derive segments by using one or more of the following job characteristics:

- Customers or markets
- Complexity of jobs
- Design features
- Job routing

Appendix B (on the enclosed CD) provides many more details along with some procedures to help you with the task of finding the FTMS.

I will give an example here to illustrate the power of the FTMS and convince you of its importance for Q-ROC formation. Also, to illustrate the application of Q-ROCs to more than just order processing, here is an example from engineering change processing.

A company had an engineering change process that was taking 45 to 60 days to complete. In brainstorming about an FTMS for engineering change requests, we came up with the following criteria: the change request involves no more than two drawings, and the change can be implemented with existing tooling. The reason for these criteria was that such requests were much simpler to review and approve. It turned out that around 50% of all the change requests fit into this FTMS, and with an appropriately designed Q-ROC and some simple cross-training, the cell could approve such a request in 1 to 2 days! Admittedly, we had solved the problem for only 50% of the changes, but think about this—if 50% of requests have their lead time reduced from 45 days to 2 days, that's still a big impact on the overall system. The next step would be to tackle some of the remaining change requests, and so on.

How to Form Effective Q-ROCs

Once you are ready with the initial FTMS choice, it is time to reorganize your operations to serve this FTMS. This is where companies often fall into the trap of not thinking outside the box. In fact this trap is embodied by another misconception from the QRM quiz: We can implement QRM by forming teams in each department (**Traditional Belief #8**).

Teams are widely used in organizational improvement efforts, but the problem with this belief is that the teams are organized within each functional department. Such a team may improve the local quality in the department but it will do little to reduce the overall MCT. In order to reduce MCT, it is necessary to break down functional walls and create a team that can process jobs through multiple functional steps in one fell swoop. Hence the QRM principle that must replace the traditional belief is: cut through functional boundaries by forming a **Quick Response Office Cell (Q-ROC)**, which is a closed-loop, collocated, dedicated multifunctional, cross-trained team responsible for the office processing of all jobs belonging to a specific Focused Target Market Segment (FTMS). The team has complete ownership of the cell's operation and the primary goal of the team is reduction of the cell's MCT (**QRM Principle #8**).

Note that this definition is consistent with the definition of a QRM Cell in Chapter 2, but this version is focused on office operations. Let's understand the importance of some of the terms in this principle. "Closed-loop" signifies that when jobs enter the Q-ROC, the team has both the expertise and the authority to complete the processing of those jobs. In fact this brings us to the second and third organizational principles, namely ownership and cross-training. As part of the formation of the Q-ROC, it is important to provide team members with expertise via cross-training, and also empower the team to make necessary decisions in order to serve the particular FTMS.

Collocation—namely physically locating the team members together in one area—is an important part of the transformation toward the QRM organization. Specifically, moving the team members out of their departments and into this new area sends a strong message to the whole organization that you will not continue with "business as usual" and you are committed to the new ways of operation. In fact, another misconception that I encounter often is, "We can implement cross-functional teams while keeping our organizational structure the way it is now." Such teams, where members still reside in their functional departments, will schedule periodic meetings in conference rooms but not really gel or accomplish the magnitude of improvements that you will see by creating a Q-ROC and collocating and dedicating people to it. To realize these improvements you really have to cut through functional boundaries and change reporting structures. To complete the organizational transformation you need to be sure that the QRM Number is the primary metric for the team, so that its focus is on constantly reducing its MCT.

The FTMS and Q-ROC Reinforce Each Other and Provide the Basis for Rethinking Processes

Identifying the FTMS and then forming a Q-ROC is not the end of the story however. The combination of FTMS and Q-ROC structure provides many additional opportunities for MCT reduction. The key here is to brainstorm together to find "whole new ways" of processing with the focus on minimizing MCT. With this new goal (instead of efficiency and cost), the cross-functional group will come up with many new ideas. Here are some pointers that will help teams in coming up with ideas for these "whole new ways":

Combine Steps

Through cross-training, one person can accomplish multiple steps currently done by several people. In fact, when forming a Q-ROC, you shouldn't assume that if the job goes to twelve different people today, then you will need twelve people in the Q-ROC. Using some of the other ideas in the two following sections along with cross-training, you might find that the Q-ROC only needs three or four people in it. Let me illustrate this with a concrete example. Consider the cost-estimating and quoting process at a company with custom sheet metal products. Part of the quoting process involves the job going from the Inside Sales Department to the Engineering Department for preliminary design, then to the Cost Estimating Department to calculate a cost, and then back to Inside Sales to add a markup and send a quote to the customer. Sometimes the Inside Sales person is not happy with the result of the magnitude of the quote ("This customer will simply not pay that much!") and sends the job back for redesign and recosting.

Now suppose the company forms a Q-ROC focused on lightweight aluminum cabinets (the FTMS). One of the team members in the Q-ROC is a design engineer who gets cross-trained in both inside-sales tasks and cost estimating. Then this person can now accomplish all three steps—not only does this save on handoffs and queue time between the steps, but also prevents iterations and rework. For instance, during the process this engineer, who knows the customer, can keep in mind what type of cost this customer will tolerate and use that to drive his or her design and quotation. You might wonder, however, how difficult it would be to train an engineer to pick up these other tasks. After all, there are people in your organization that have taken 5 or even 10 years to become experts in cost estimating, sales, or other such tasks. So how could you easily train a new person to do this without it taking years? The answer is contained in one acronym: FTMS! One of the keys to a Q-ROC's performance is that it is focused on a limited set of jobs, and this allows it to simplify the processing steps and also more easily cross-train people. For instance, in a Cost Estimating Department that handles all the jobs in the company, people need to be trained on a wide variety of cost-estimating issues. But for the example given here, the engineer needs to estimate only the cost of a limited variety of aluminum cabinets (possibly with limited features as defined by the FTMS), and this could be learned with a few weeks of cross-training, not years.

Eliminate Steps

Again, by taking advantage of the FTMS definition, you will find that processing steps can be eliminated altogether. In most organizations, extra steps are added over time because of problems that were experienced with specific orders. ("We got killed by the change in some components' pricing. From now on, every job needs to be checked by the purchasing manager to avoid this problem …" and so on.) However, once the FTMS has been identified, you will find that many steps simply do not apply to this subset or else they can be eliminated because of the cross-training and expertise that will be contained in the Q-ROC team.

Redesign Steps

Encourage brainstorming sessions where people think out of the box about new ways to process the jobs in the FTMS, once again keeping in mind that speed is the goal. Continuing with the example of the sheet metal products company, traditionally quotes are cost estimated in detail, taking into account all the manufacturing processes that would be required to form the features on the requested product. However, after forming the FTMS for certain limited types of aluminum cabinets, the team might be able to come up with simple quoting tables based on a few key features of the cabinets. Then the cost-estimating task would simply be replaced by a table lookup by the design engineer. If needed, this process could be refined by allowing the engineer to include a few add-on costs based on specific customer requirements. In any case, the detailed cost-estimating step would be redesigned and result in a much shorter MCT for the Q-ROC. Managers are sometimes reluctant to give up detailed cost estimating in favor of these simpler estimating methods. "We could lose our shirt if we don't carefully cost out our jobs!" In reality, there are many reasons why this won't necessarily happen. First, regardless of how carefully your experienced estimator costs out a job, many changes are possible between the time of the costing and the actual production: material prices could change, a supplier could be late in delivery, the production process could take longer than expected due to tooling failures, an experienced operator could be sick and the job might be done by a novice, and so on. So no matter how well the cost estimator did his or her job, the real world will intervene and things will change. Second, by getting more quotes out fast to customers you will land more orders, and even if your margins are not quite as high in some cases, at the very least you will be gaining market share and volume, and better still, you might even make up with higher margins for some jobs. By reducing the time spent in estimating and also the time spent overall in the quoting process, you will also reduce your operating costs and positively impact your profitability.

Provide Continuous Flow of Work

When jobs need to flow through multiple departments, work is often done in batches. One reason for this is just the fact that jobs sit in "out" boxes and get moved only periodically. As we saw in the previous chapter, large batches can result in longer MCTs. This is just as true in the office as it is in manufacturing. First, there is the time that jobs sit in the first department, waiting for the batch to be built up. Then, after the batch arrives at the next department, the jobs are processed one at a time, so jobs in the pile have to wait until the jobs ahead of them are done—again adding to MCT. In a Q-ROC these problems are eliminated for two reasons: first, through cross-training, one person can accomplish multiple steps, so a single job gets taken through multiple steps without waiting; and second, since people are collocated, the physical proximity means that team members can pass jobs on to the next person immediately, and in many cases even let them know with a verbal comment or other physical cue that the job has been handed to them. Thus in a Q-ROC there is a built-in structure to support continuous flow of work—all that's needed is for the team to be aware that this is important and they should be motivated to support this flow.

Take Advantage of the Latest Information Technology and Tools

If you are wondering whether jobs need to be physically passed between team members, this is an important question! If your processes were put in place a few years ago, it might be time to reexamine if today's technology would allow you to do these steps electronically or even differently—again, revisit the "whole new ways" idea. For instance, information stored on shared network drives may eliminate the need for orders to be physically passed from person to person. Or availability of information on Web sites may allow the team to get data that previously required a different department to be involved (for example, instead of asking Purchasing to get information on a component's cost, a team member could look up a price on a supplier's Web site). Note that such redesigning of steps may require changes in organizational policies (for instance, who is allowed to look at cost information), and upper management may have to get involved to cut through such organizational red tape in order for the Q-ROC to operate successfully. Another such instance is different information systems used by different departments—once multiple functions are incorporated in the Q-ROC this will raise issues about compatibility (and even ownership) of systems and data. Management should be prepared to deal with such issues as they arise and keep in mind the goal of reducing lead time and gaining competitive advantage.

Overcome Traditional Mind-Sets

In order to support the Q-ROC, management must also overcome other traditional mindset issues. Key among these are:

- **Beware of the "utilization" argument.** Management must ensure that the Q-ROC has sufficient infrastructure and resources to enable fast flow through the cell. For example, if management finds it hard to justify an additional phone line and fax machine, or computer, because they wouldn't be utilized much of the time it should be reminded of the landing gear example. The goal of the cell is to ensure quick response to satisfy larger business goals, and these resources need to be justified in the broader context.
- **Eliminate approval steps.** Once the Q-ROC structure is in place along with the cross-training and ownership, management must also eliminate traditional approval and control systems. Not only do these create additional choke points in the flow, but they also take away from the ownership of the team; in fact they give the message that management does not trust the team to do a good job. Ownership does not mean giving unlimited authority to the Q-ROC. Management can set predefined boundaries, and outside these boundaries the team will need to seek approval. But for all jobs that fall within the boundaries, the team should have the authority to complete the job without seeking any approval. For instance, a Q-ROC that is involved in cost estimating and quoting could be told that any quotes up to a certain dollar amount can go out without further approval, but quotes above a certain amount need to be reviewed by a manager. This is entirely appropriate. To summarize, ownership does not mean unlimited authority, but rather, it means full authority within prespecified limits.
- **Simplify planning and control.** As the organization gets transformed into cells, management needs to simplify or even eliminate centralized project planning and control systems. These project management systems were created over time because jobs that went through many functional departments were repeatedly late—the irony of this

is that often companies would create yet another department, called the Project Management Department! With the simplified structure of the cells along with ownership within the cells, central management of jobs becomes unnecessary.

As an even bolder step toward the cellular structure cutting across functional lines, management can consider collocating office and manufacturing cells! This is possible if the FTMS for both the office cell and manufacturing cell can be the same. In some organizations, a job from an office cell could go to one of many shop floor cells. However, in other organizations, a direct correspondence can be created between an office cell and a manufacturing cell. In such cases, I have seen the office cell actually located on the shop floor, next to the manufacturing cell. The Q-ROC is usually situated in a walled enclosure to provide sound-proofing from the shop floor machines, but with plenty of windows to allow visual contact with the manufacturing cell. This proximity results in numerous benefits. For instance, during the quoting process, if a team member in the Q-ROC has a question about the capability of the machines, she can walk out to the manufacturing cell and ask one of the team members if the machine would be able to perform the particular operation. Similarly, if one of the machinists has a question about a blueprint for a part that is being made, he can walk right into the Q-ROC and ask one of the engineers there to answer the question. Needless to say, this collocation also involves a big mind-set change, not only by management but also the employees since the people in the Q-ROC will need to move from the traditional office building to residing in the glass-walled enclosure on the shop floor. While this may be met with some resistance initially, in the long run it has been my experience that both the office and the manufacturing team will see the benefits of the collocation and realize that it has made their jobs less stressful and improved their performance.

Additional Challenges in Reorganizing Office Operations

I should add a final comment about the principles in this section. The preceding principles form the foundation for quick response in office operations, but are not necessarily sufficient for success. Companies have implemented these principles only to find that lead time reduction has been less than they expected. Why? There are three main reasons for limited success:

- **Lack of use of system dynamics principles to complement the organizational principles.** At the beginning of the previous chapter, I gave you several examples of companies that formed manufacturing cells but still had poor lead time performance, and the reason was that they did not take into account system dynamics. The same is true for office cells. As a very simple example, if you create a Q-ROC but do not have sufficient capacity in the cell, then even the best teamwork and ownership will not be able to achieve short lead times. In designing the Q-ROC, keep in mind the main system dynamics principles, which are: (1) strategically plan for spare capacity; (2) reduce variability in terms of both job arrivals and time for tasks performed; (3) as far as possible, convert multiple tasks from being sequential to overlapping or parallel; (4) minimize batching—in the office context, this often means that if you create templates or standardized forms people will do the task right away rather than collecting like tasks to be done later. Let me elaborate more on one issue, that of capacity. Manufacturing companies usually have lots of data about production times and engage in some sort of capacity planning for the shop floor. But these same companies almost never manage capacity in the office, and in fact lack data about how long it takes to do various office operations. It is never too late to start doing this. You saw in Chapter 3 the huge impact of capacity utilization on lead times, so poor capacity management can result in disasters. It is not necessary to invest in very sophisticated systems though. You should understand that rough capacity management is better than no capacity control. Start creating ways for Q-ROCs to understand their capacity and then anticipate and plan ahead for it. Some simple visual tools, such as the POLCA system described later, can also help to accomplish this capacity management without needing to invest in expensive systems.
- **Use of obsolete performance measures.** To support the goals of the Q-ROC, it is important that management emphasize time-based measures, such as the QRM Number, and deemphasize measures such as utilization and efficiency. Otherwise team members will revert to the traditional mind-set as well, such as batching jobs to increase their efficiency numbers.
- **A traditional management mind-set.** If management continues to keep the traditional mind-set, there will be ongoing obstacles to transforming your office operations. The formation and successful

operation of Q-ROCs require breaking through existing structures, rethinking procedures and processes and who is allowed to do what, eliminating approval steps, and more—in sum, it requires challenging norms and policies that have been in use for many years. If management's mind-set continues to support these traditional norms, then the QRM projects will have limited success or even stall altogether. The next chapter discusses this issue, as well as how to create the right management structure to support implementation of QRM.

Although there are many challenges to implementing QRM in office operations, a major advantage that this has over applying QRM to the shop floor is that moving people and desks is much less costly than moving machines and creating shop floor cells. Companies that have overcome the challenges and reorganized into Q-ROCs in their office have seen amazing results. One such company is described next.

A Case Study: Q-ROCs Rock at Alexandria Extrusion Company

Alexandria Extrusion Company (AEC) based in Alexandria, Minnesota (about 140 miles northwest of Minneapolis), makes precision aluminum extrusions. AEC is a medium-size business with about 300 employees, and it specializes in providing custom aluminum extrusions with quick response times. In 2002 Tom Schabel, president and owner of AEC, attended a QRM seminar and decided to implement QRM as AEC's competitive strategy. One of the first areas targeted for QRM was the office environment, in particular, the time it took from receipt of a purchase order (PO) for a new item until the PO had been acknowledged to the customer confirming the price and the ship date. This time was typically 10 to 12 days and consumed a significant amount of the total lead time expected by the customer. Prior to learning about QRM, AEC had tried several team-based approaches to shortening this lead time but with no significant improvements. The underlying reasons for the lack of results were, first, the functional organizational structure was not altered (the whole process involved eleven handoffs between six different departments); and, second, there was a traditional cost-based mind-set and no awareness of time-based thinking. After learning about QRM, Tom Schabel decided to conduct QRM training for the management and key employees. Based on the QRM principles learned during the training, AEC analyzed its operations and decided to form four Q-ROCs, each one formed around an FTMS based on similar products, similar processing, and similar quoting and engineering processes. (The information here is based on a presentation entitled "Q-ROCs Rock!" by Rick Jones, Genny LeBrun, and Stuart Schmidt of AEC, given at the QRM 2007 International Conference on Quick Response Manufacturing, Madison, Wisconsin, June 2007.)

As we have seen from many QRM implementations, these Q-ROCs reduced the upfront lead time by more than 50%, to as little as 3 days in many cases, and 5 days at the most. But much more happened, and here I want to tell you about the unexpected results. The Q-ROCs produced many process and cost improvements. They resulted in a substantial increase in capacity, leading to a record amount of business in their first year of implementation with no additional people in the office. But most of all, it was the recognition that they got from the customers that showed that the Q-ROCs really "rocked"! AEC received numerous positive comments from its customers about the impact of the Q-ROCs on their responsiveness. A concrete measure of the customers' happiness was that in the first year AEC received three supplier-of-the-year awards from major customers.

In addition to transforming its office operations, Alexandria Extrusion has implemented QRM in many other areas of its business including pursuing the relentless reduction of batch sizes over time, and implementing the POLCA system for material control on the shop floor. Overall, QRM has enabled AEC to grow significantly over the past 6 years while also lowering its costs and increasing its profitability. As stated by Tom Schabel, "QRM gives us a definite edge over our competition. With the economic downturn in 2008 and 2009, the overall market for AEC's products shrank by 50%, yet AEC was able to grow and expand during these two years. Without a doubt, QRM was the significant driver behind our success. Our lead time reduction has created a new benchmark for lead time in the aluminum extrusion industry. A new customer recently told me that QRM was a factor in why our company was selected as a supplier."

RESTRUCTURE YOUR MATERIAL-PLANNING SYSTEM TO SUPPORT QRM

MRP, MRP II, and ERP systems are widely used for material planning and scheduling in manufacturing enterprises. Although these systems have many useful functions to support the enterprise, they are not helpful in reducing your MCT. Indeed, another common misconception about the capability of these systems is the following: Installing a Material Requirements Planning (MRP or ERP) system will help in reducing lead times (**Traditional Belief #5**).

In fact, quite the opposite—MRP systems can result in another Response Time Spiral of increasing lead times and growing MCT. The reason stems from the structure of the planning logic used in these systems. Consider a product that needs ten different operations. Based on the ship date for the end product, the MRP system attempts to schedule a start date for each operation. In order to calculate this start date, it needs to know the lead time for each operation. This lead time is not calculated by the system, but rather, it needs to be specified by the Planning Department ahead of time. Since, at the time the lead times are being set in the MRP system, the planners don't know the actual workload that will hit a particular department in a particular week, they have to enter worst-case lead times for each operation. Why is this? I will illustrate the answer via an example.

Suppose that Natalie is a planner who is responsible for the planning and scheduling of certain parts. Some of Natalie's parts go through the Welding Department, which supplies the welded parts to a final assembly operation. If the parts do not arrive on time, that will hold up the assembly and possibly result in late shipments to customers. Now let's say that based on past performance, Natalie knows that jobs can usually get through the Welding Department in 3 or 4 days, but if the department is backed up with work or if some of the welding equipment is down, then it can take as much as 2 weeks to get through Welding. Keep in mind that Natalie is responsible for making sure that her parts get to downstream operations on time, and this is an important part of her annual performance review. Since she doesn't want to risk the parts being late to assembly, what choice does Natalie have but to put in 2 weeks for the lead time for the welding operation? So we have ended up with a worst-case lead time number for Welding. Now multiply this effect by 10, since there are ten operations. If on average the lead time for each operation is 2 days, but the worst case is 10 days as in the welding example, then a 20-day average total lead time becomes inflated to a 100-day total planning lead time in MRP. In other words, the first operation will be started 100 days before the ship date. With such long planning lead times for this and other parts, the organization will now experience the Response Time Spiral described in Chapter 2, and the lead times will keep getting longer.

So what is the solution? Some experts suggest that you invest in more sophisticated planning and scheduling systems to complement your MRP system. Others suggest scrapping the MRP logic altogether, and replacing it with more advanced planning systems or Kanban methods. The good news is that to support your QRM implementation, none of these drastic approaches is necessary. Also, in the next section I will explain why Kanban won't serve our needs either. Instead, a few simple fixes to your MRP system will go a long way toward supporting your QRM strategy. Thus you can build on the system you already have, rather than having to replace it. The QRM principle to replace the traditional belief is thus: Align your MRP structure with your QRM strategy. After you restructure the organization into QRM Cells, use MRP for higher level planning of material flow from suppliers and between cells. Complement this with POLCA, the QRM material control method that coordinates flows between cells in order to meet delivery dates (**QRM Principle #5**).

Implementing High-Level MRP

Essentially, you need to restructure your MRP system and your planning methods in the following ways. Note that most of these principles are relatively simple to implement, and require primarily a mind-set change—in particular, you will not need to invest in any complex systems design or programming. The key is to understand that in the QRM organization, you use the MRP system to provide high-level planning and coordination of materials from external suppliers and across internal cells in order to meet delivery dates. I call this High-Level MRP, or HL/MRP (see Figure 4.4). The key ideas of HL/MRP are as follows:

- Start by restructuring your organization into QRM Cells as already described in earlier sections of this book.

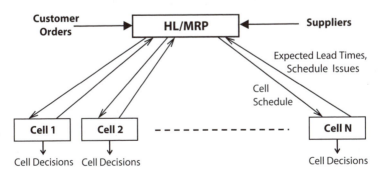

FIGURE 4.4
High-level MRP system.

- As you create cells for various parts, also use this opportunity to rethink bills of material for this new structure of production, always with a goal of reducing MCT. In particular, you should rethink design, material choices, and make/buy decisions to *flatten* bills of material and eliminate operations. You might have to battle conventional cost-based thinking to implement some of these changes, but you should use many of the arguments presented in this book (such as the design change example in Chapter 1, illustrated in Figure 1.10 there).

- Use the HL/MRP system to plan the flow of materials from suppliers and across cells in order to meet delivery dates as follows. The system should manage stock levels and reorder material using its standard logic. It should also derive start dates using the standard logic by beginning with the delivery date and performing backward scheduling based on lead times. However, lead times in the system should be set at the cell level, not at the operation level. For instance, if a part goes through six operations within one cell, in the standard MRP system this would be represented by six steps with six lead times. Now, with the HL/MRP system, the entire set of operations performed in the cell would be represented by one step with one lead time, which would be the planned lead time for that cell.

- Note in particular that you will no longer use MRP to micromanage the operations within cells; this is in keeping with the QRM concept that a cell team has ownership of operations within the cell. In the preceding example of the part with six operations, the team would simply be informed of the expected start and finish dates for the part and it would manage the details of how and when the six operations would be performed to meet those expectations. Since cells will now be responsible for their schedules, teams should also be provided with simple capacity-planning tools and trained in their use as part of the cross-training program so they can anticipate bottlenecks and put strategies in place to manage them.

- As the cell teams become more experienced at managing their schedules and capacity, then by looking at their upcoming loads they can take a proactive role in communicating with the planners as conditions change. For instance, they can suggest that work be reallocated, schedules be adjusted, or their lead times be changed. This will help to keep the lead times and schedules in the HL/MRP system more realistic and accurate, and prevent some of the MRP-related problems just described and in Chapter 3.

- If a part needs to go through multiple cells, the POLCA system described in the next section is used to coordinate the flow between cells. Even with the best planning, real-world disturbances such as machine failures or unexpected orders will still occur, and POLCA helps to ensure that cells adjust their production priorities to meet end-item delivery schedules.

Understanding Why HL/MRP Will Work Better than Standard MRP

Since the QRM approach of using this HL/MRP system still depends on much of the standard MRP logic (e.g., assigning lead times and back scheduling from delivery dates) you might well ask: "Why will this HL/MRP approach work well when you have just told me all the reasons that traditional MRP systems fail?" There are several factors that ensure that the HL/MRP system will work better, and I will illustrate them with an example.

Consider a company that makes many different electronic products for industrial use, where we will look at the production of industrial controllers. The company is originally organized in a traditional functional structure, which therefore governs the flow of products as well as the MRP logic (see Figure 4.5). The controllers consist of two main subassemblies: a sheet metal enclosure and a printed circuit board (PCB). The routing of the enclosure takes it through six functional departments (such as shearing, punching, and bending), while the PCB goes through five departments (such as through-hole insertion, wave soldering, and surface mount assembly). These two components then come together and go through three final assembly departments, at which point the product is completed.

As the company reorganizes its operations using QRM strategy, several QRM Cells are formed. In particular, relevant to the flow of the product in our example are three cells as follows. The enclosures will now be made in a "Small Steel Enclosures" cell, which has as its FTMS all enclosures

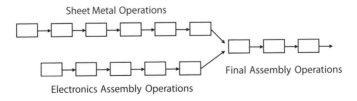

Sheet Metal Operations

Final Assembly Operations

Electronics Assembly Operations

FIGURE 4.5
Traditional MRP routing for production of industrial controllers.

made from stainless steel and smaller than some specific dimensions (this includes the enclosures for our product, as well as for several other products). Another FTMS is identified as large PCBs, and a QRM Cell is created for these. Finally, it is decided that all types of controllers will be assembled in one final assembly area and a QRM Cell is created for this set of assembly and test operations. Hence the industrial controllers line of products now has the flow shown in Figure 4.6. Note that in the HL/MRP system the planning is done at the cell level, so that the multiple steps inside the cell have been aggregated into one step for each cell.

Comparing this figure with the original organization in Figure 4.5 helps to illustrate the reasons why the QRM approach using HL/MRP will work better:

- The first and most obvious reason, as is visible from the two figures, is that while the longest flow path in Figure 4.5 consists of nine routing steps, the longest path in Figure 4.6 is only two steps. So even if the planner needs to add some safety time to the lead times for each step in the HL/MRP system as well, the back scheduling will add together at most two padded lead times, as opposed to nine padded lead times in the original system.
- The previous effect is magnified further when we also consider the impact of variability in lead times. Let's say that in the original system each department had an average lead time of 3 days, but due to high variability in departmental performance, the planners actually used an MRP lead time of 7 days for each department (I explained the reasons for this with the example of the planner Natalie). With nine routing steps in the longest path, this meant that the total planned lead time for industrial controllers in the old system was 63 days. After implementing the QRM Cells, let's say the three cells

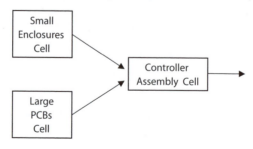

FIGURE 4.6
QRM approach using HL/MRP routing for production of industrial controllers.

under consideration are able to achieve an average lead time of 2 days each. In addition, thanks to the ownership by the cell teams there is little variability in performance and the lead times are quite reliable, so the planners feel quite comfortable with adding just 1 day of safety time to each of the lead times, giving a planned lead time of 3 days for each cell in the HL/MRP system. Since the longest flow path involves only two steps, the total planned lead time for industrial controllers is now only 6 days. This example points out that not only are the number of steps reduced with the new structure, but also the amount of padding needed at each step is reduced. These benefits multiply fast: in our example, while the old system had 4½ times more steps than the new one, the planned lead time in the old system was actually 10 times longer.

- The use of POLCA to coordinate and control intercell flow also helps the overall product flow stay on schedule and thus minimizes the amount of safety time the planners need to use. I explain this effect in more detail when I describe POLCA in the next section. Unlike a Kanban (or "pull") system, which attempts to replace the MRP functions with its own material planning, you will appreciate the fact that POLCA actually uses your existing MRP system and builds on it to make it more effective.

Not only will the new system have a much shorter planned lead time, but this lead time will also be more reliable. This is not just the result of using the HL/MRP system approach, but rather the combination of the new system along with the QRM strategies of cells, teams, ownership, and POLCA that reinforce each other to get the desired effect. This illustrates a strength of QRM, which you will realize as you understand more of the total QRM picture, namely that the whole is greater than the sum of its parts: the QRM approaches to each part of the enterprise complement and strengthen each other to result in enterprise-wide performance improvements that actually exceed the sum of the remarkable results already achieved in each area.

POLCA—THE SHOP FLOOR MATERIAL CONTROL STRATEGY TO SUPPORT QRM

An MRP system by its very name indicates that it is a planning system. When a plan is executed, then that plan, no matter how good, still needs to be managed and fine-tuned. As the real world intervenes, there will be unanticipated customer orders and schedule changes as well as unexpected problems and events. You need a control system to cope with these changes and help you modify and execute your plan as best as possible. POLCA is just such a system, designed to work within the QRM structure of cells, teams, ownership, and the HL/MRP system.

Why Kanban (Pull) Won't Work in the QRM Context

Before I describe POLCA, you might well be wondering why a new system is needed. In particular, since Kanban systems are designed for shop floor coordination and control and have been very successful, why not just use Kanban within the QRM framework of cells and MRP? To answer this question, observe first that Kanban was designed as part of Toyota's production system, which worked in the context of high-volume production of similar products and with fairly stable demand. More specifically, to see how these origins impact the way Kanban works, I need to go into a few of the basic principles on which Kanban is based.

Takt Time Issues

A key starting point for design of a Kanban system is calculating the takt time for each operation. This is defined as the cycle time within which that operation must be completed in order to keep up with the average rate of sales. By keeping all operations working at just under their takt times, the Kanban system creates a balanced system and good flow through the shop floor. If preliminary analysis shows that any operations exceed their takt times, then the system needs to be reconfigured to bring them all within the takt time: for example, the operations could be redesigned, additional resources could be allocated, or even the product design might be modified. However, note that all the takt time calculations are based on the average rate of sales. With relatively stable demand, this average provides a reasonable number to work with. On the other hand, if demand or product mix or both vary a lot from week to week, so that bottlenecks can also vary significantly from one week to the next, then the takt time numbers are not meaningful in any given week. In other words, all the reconfigurations done based on takt times would be essentially ineffective as each week's demand arrived.

Pull System Issues

The second key feature of a Kanban system—as described by its common name of "pull" —is that parts are "pulled" through the factory as they are used up in downstream operations. We can understand this operation clearly by starting from the finished product. When a container of finished goods is shipped out of the warehouse, a signal is sent to the previous operation to restock that container. That operation has the partially completed material for this product waiting in its stock area, and when it draws a container of this material to work on it, it then sends a signal to its previous operation to resupply that material. These signals are often in the form of physical cards called Kanban cards. Each such signal therefore needs to specify both a part number and a quantity that needs to be made. Thus for the Kanban system to work, you need to have these partly completed products stocked in containers at each stage of the manufacturing system. If you make a small variety of parts and all with relatively high demand, then this system keeps the material moving; it is simple to implement, and it works very well.

However, consider what happens to the pull approach when you have a large variety of products and many of them have very low annual demand. Suppose a company makes axles for nonautomotive applications, such as for construction and mining equipment. Let's say this company stocks in its finished goods a container with six axles of a certain type, and that typically it gets an order from a distribution center once a year for one of these containers. Let's see what happens when this order arrives. The container is shipped and a Kanban signal is sent to the previous operation. Within a couple of days, the previous operation completes the production of the six axles and restocks the warehouse. Now these axles are going to sit in the warehouse for about a year before another order is received. In other words you have an inventory turnover rate of only once a year for this product! If most of your products have low demand, then your overall inventory turnover is also going to be very low, perhaps two or three times a year at best. In an era when management expects to achieve turnover rates of 20 or more times a year, this would be atrocious. But it is actually worse than this, because not only are the finished axles sitting in the warehouse, but along the whole flow path of the axles there are partly completed products sitting at various stocking points throughout the shop floor, waiting for a pull signal from an upstream operation so that they can be worked on and sent to that operation. This is not an unknown phenomenon; in fact people that design Kanban systems know that these inventories will be needed throughout the shop floor and they even have a name for these intermediate stocks: they are called "supermarkets." When the production volume is high, there is no need for concern about supermarkets because the items move through the supermarket quickly and the inventory turnover rate is high enough. Thus Kanban works well in these environments; but in low-volume environments, instead of eliminating waste it actually creates more waste.

Difficulties with Custom or New Products

As a final point, now consider the same company and suppose it receives an order for a custom-engineered axle for a large mining machine. How would the Kanban system work in this situation? It won't work at all. You can understand this by realizing that Kanban is a replenishment system: You begin by shipping finished goods and then sending a signal to have them replenished—but you can't have something in finished goods if it has never been made before; in fact it hasn't even been engineered yet. Indeed, at each step of the whole Kanban shop floor operation, you pick partially completed material from your stocking point and then ask for that material to be replenished. So this flow cannot operate for a custom-engineered product from the point at which customized operations begin and onward.

In Chapter 1, I explain the concept of strategic variability and how you can take advantage of this to gain competitive advantage. Kanban was simply not designed to operate in environments of high variability or custom products. Thus, to control material flow on the shop floor in the QRM organization we need a system that works well in the context of low-volume or customized products and also in the context of the cellular structure that we have implemented. POLCA is designed specifically to meet these needs. Here I will give you the main idea so you can understand how it overcomes the preceding issues with the Kanban system and also appreciate the additional benefits of using POLCA to support your QRM strategy; further details of how POLCA works are in Appendix E (see the enclosed CD).

Companies that have complex products with many fabricated components, or products that require a very large number of operations, find that they cannot make their end products from start to finish in one QRM Cell—such a cell would be so large as to be unwieldy and the team size would also be too large to enable good teamwork. Thus many companies organize into multiple QRM Cells feeding each other. For instance you could have several fabrication cells, each designed around different types of components, and these cells could feed multiple subassembly cells, which would in turn feed final assembly cells. I will describe how POLCA would work in such a situation, and that will enable you to see its key features and benefits.

POLCA stands for **Paired-cell Overlapping Loops of Cards with Authorization**. Each of these terms signifies one of the key features of POLCA, and in the rest of this section I will go over each of these key features.

Paired-cell Loops of Cards

In POLCA, if material flows between any two cells, let's say from Cell A to Cell B, then these cells are connected by a POLCA loop (see Figure 4.7). This loop contains a number of cards called POLCA cards that circulate in the loop; these cards are specific to this loop and are labeled based on the origin and destination cell; in this case they would be called A/B cards. When Cell A is scheduled to start a job that is destined for Cell B, it needs to have an A/B card available in order to launch the job into Cell A. If the card is available, the job is started and the card is kept with the job or with its paperwork, to signify that the card is associated with that job. When Cell A completes the job, it sends the job along with the A/B card to Cell B. I'll get to Cell B's operation in a moment, but for now just note that when Cell B finishes working on this job, it sends the job on to the next cell and sends the A/B card back to Cell A. Thus you can see the first key point of the POLCA system— the card coming back from Cell B essentially conveys the message "We

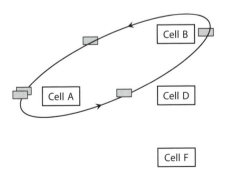

FIGURE 4.7
POLCA loop between Cell A and Cell B with five circulating A/B POLCA cards.

finished one of the jobs you sent us; you can send us another." In other words, returning POLCA cards signify the availability of capacity in downstream cells.

Here I'd like to point out a very important difference between POLCA and Kanban. Kanban is an *inventory* signal: the signal gets triggered when a certain quantity of parts is used up, and the signal tells the previous operation to make up that inventory by supplying that quantity of parts. On the other hand, POLCA is a *capacity* signal: the signal is triggered when a job is completed, and the signal tells the previous cell that it is okay to send another job to this cell. This difference between an inventory signal and a capacity signal is in fact very significant and underlies why POLCA works for low-volume and custom parts while Kanban is not suited to these environments.

Authorization

The second feature of POLCA concerns the issue of how Cell A decides which job to start next. Remember that in QRM you have an HL/MRP system that plans your material flow. Thus, based on the ship dates of end products, this system back schedules the requirements of materials and calculates the start dates for each job at each cell. In POLCA we call these dates authorization dates because we want to signify that the cell is authorized to start the job from the HL/MRP viewpoint, but it also needs to follow additional POLCA rules before it can actually start the job. Essentially, jobs with start dates of today or earlier are authorized, while jobs with dates of tomorrow or later are not authorized.

Dispatch List

After the HL/MRP system performs its calculations, the system compiles a Dispatch List (say once a day, or once a shift) for each cell, which shows all the jobs that have not yet been started by that cell, ordered by authorization date (earliest date on the top of the list)—see Figure 4.8 for an example. The shading in the figure separates the authorized jobs from the rest; since the date in the example is January 15, jobs with dates of the 15th or earlier are authorized, while jobs with dates of January 16 or later are not authorized.

The cell team's decision process for picking which job to start is simple: take the first authorized job on the list; since it has the earliest authorization

Charles Casing Company — Dispatch List			
Cell Name: Cell A Date: January 15, 2010			
Job ID	Authorization Date	Next Cell	Additional Job Data...
NR07	January 13	D	...
R2D2	January 15	B	...
C3P0	January 15	D	...
AK08	January 16	F	...
DR06	January 17	B	...
...	...	...	...
...	...	...	...

FIGURE 4.8
Example of dispatch list used with POLCA.

date it is the most important one to work on. For example, the dispatch list in Figure 4.8 for January 15 still contains a job with an authorization date of January 13; this job should have been started two days ago and so it needs to be worked on as soon as possible. Next, the team looks up where this job is going after their cell (this information is also supplied as part of the Dispatch List in POLCA, as shown in Figure 4.8). The Dispatch List shows that the job is going to Cell D next. Then the Cell A team checks to see if they have an A/D POLCA card. (Typically, each team will have a bulletin board where it organizes all the POLCA cards currently available to that cell.) If there is an A/D card available, the POLCA card is attached to the job's paperwork and the job is launched into the cell. If there is no A/D card available, then the POLCA rule is that the team must skip this job for now and go to the next job on the dispatch list.

So why is a capacity signal needed at all, and why might it be beneficial? Suppose there are five cards in the A/D loop—using the terminology of the POLCA system we would say there are five A/D POLCA cards. (The number of cards is calculated to keep the system working smoothly; this calculation is explained in Appendix E on the enclosed CD.) Now suppose that the dispatch list for Cell A tells it to start a job that is destined for Cell D. However, when the team looks at its bulletin board, it sees that there are no A/D cards available. What does this tell us? This means that all five cards are in use with other jobs, so these jobs either are still being worked on in Cell D, or are on their way to Cell D. Essentially, either Cell D is backed up with work, or there is enough work already on its way to Cell D. In either case, sending another job to Cell D will not be productive as it won't be able to work on it in the near future and the job will just sit, adding to the WIP and the MCT. Like sending more cars into a traffic jam, sending more jobs into a bottleneck resource is not a good idea! On the other hand, there may be other cells that are waiting for work from Cell A. For example, if the next job on the list is destined for Cell B, and there are A/B POLCA cards available, this means that if Cell A works on this job there is a good chance that B will also be ready to work on it and the job will keep moving. So skipping the job destined for Cell D and working on the job for Cell B instead is in fact a good idea from the point of view of the overall system flow.

Hence you see another key feature of the POLCA system. POLCA cards ensure that upstream cells work on jobs that will go somewhere instead of working on jobs that will end up just sitting at another bottleneck. In other words, POLCA ensures the most effective use of your capacity at each moment of time.

Strict Scheduling Rules

Suppose there is no A/D POLCA card available to the cell team. Then it needs to skip to the next job that is destined for Cell B, so the team needs an A/B POLCA card to start this job. Suppose also that no A/B POLCA card is available at this time. Then the team will have to skip this job as well and go to the third job. In fact, looking at Figure 4.8 you see that the team will have to skip a total of three jobs on the Dispatch List because the third job is going to Cell D and you already know that no A/D POLCA card is currently available. Now let's say the next job on the Dispatch List has an authorization date of January 16, it is destined for Cell F, and an A/F POLCA card is present on the team's bulletin board. Remember that in this example, the current date is January 15. The rule in POLCA is that even though the right card is available, this job cannot be started until January 16.

So, to clarify the scheduling rules in POLCA, in order to start a job three conditions need to be satisfied: the first and obvious condition is that the job or material needs to have arrived at the cell; the second is that the authorization date needs to be today or earlier; and the third is that the right POLCA card needs to be available. In fact, since the three jobs with earlier dates had to be skipped due to lack of POLCA cards, and this job cannot be started yet, this will mean that the team cannot start any jobs at this moment in time. This is important to note. In a typical shop floor operation, if people don't have work to do, a supervisor will look ahead in the schedule and try to start some jobs even if they get made much earlier than needed. In POLCA the rule is clear: all jobs with authorization dates of today's date or earlier are authorized, while all other jobs of dates in the future are not authorized and cannot be started.

Of course, the preceding situation in Cell A would make traditional management or supervisors very uneasy. "Just because of this darn POLCA system we implemented, we now have five people in Cell A standing around doing nothing—how can that possibly be good for our company?" While at first glance it would seem that this complaint has merit, in actual fact there are several reasons why these rules in POLCA have resulted in better operations for many companies even though there are times when the preceding situation occurs on the shop floor.

Every time you put capacity into a job that is not needed, you do three bad things: you steal capacity from another job that might have needed it; you create more WIP; and you add to your MCT. The last two reasons are obvious, but if people are standing around, how could you steal capacity from another job? To see the answer, remember that the team skipped three jobs that were authorized but did not have POLCA cards available. Suppose the first of these jobs had an authorization date of January 13. That means it should have been started 2 days ago. Let's say that since the team is idle and it sees that the right POLCA card is available for the job with the authorization date of January 16, it decides to start this job anyway. The first machine for this job has a 2-hour setup, and just as the team finishes the setup and starts machining the first piece of the job, the right POLCA card for the January 13 job shows up and this job also needs to be started on that same machine. Now what will the team do? Having spent 2 hours on a setup, it is unlikely that the team will stop the job on that machine and tear down the setup and redo a new 2-hour setup for the January 13 job. More likely is the scenario that the team will finish the January 16 job and then start the January 13 job. If the January 16 job takes most of the shift to finish and the January 13 job cannot be started until the next day, what has just happened? A job that was 2 days late is now going to be at least 3 days late, while a job that was not needed is going to sit on the shop floor for an extra day.

I will end the discussion of the idle team with one last observation. I pointed out in Chapter 3 that management needs to rethink its concept of "idle" workers. As mentioned in that chapter, when a team doesn't have specific production jobs to work on, there are many other useful things the team can do—spend time in cross-training, study a setup in order to come up with ideas for setup time reduction, engage in preventive-maintenance tasks, and other improvement activities. In fact, if there is never any nonproduction time, when can a team engage in any of these continuous improvement activities? Teams need to be coached in the fact that they can use these periods of time productively, so that these opportunities are not lost. Viewed this way, management will no longer label the situation in Cell A as "idle" time, but see it as an integral part of the total QRM strategy.

Overlapping Loops

The remaining portion of the POLCA acronym has to do with the term "overlapping." Let's return to the first example of the job going from Cell A to Cell B and consider what happens when A completes the job. At this point the job along with the A/B POLCA card move on to Cell B. Suppose also that the next cell for this job after Cell B is Cell G, which implies that there is a B/G POLCA loop as well (see Figure 4.9). Now, note that each cell goes through exactly the same scheduling logic as just described, so when the job arrives at Cell B, the team will need to do the following for this job: it must wait for the job to be authorized if it isn't already, and all other jobs above it on the Dispatch List should already have been started or be waiting for POLCA cards; then it must check if a B/G POLCA card is available; if both these conditions are met, then the B/G POLCA card is allotted to the job and the job can be started in Cell B. However, remember that the job also arrived with an A/B POLCA card, and that card will not be sent back to Cell A until the job has been finished by Cell B.

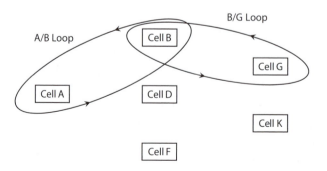

FIGURE 4.9
Illustration of overlapping loops in POLCA.

Why not send the A/B card back as soon as Cell B starts the job and puts the B/G POLCA with the job? In fact that is how Kanban works—you send the signal back as soon as you pick the material for the job. But in POLCA it is critical that the card be sent back only when the destination cell has completed the job. Why? Because POLCA is a capacity signal. Since QRM works in the context of higher variability and jobs with differing work content and requirements, we don't want a cell to send any signal until it is completely finished with a particular job.

If you think of the job that just got launched into Cell B, this job is carrying the A/B card with it already, and in addition it now has the B/G card allotted to it. So while it is being worked on in Cell B, the job will have two POLCA cards with it. Thinking this through, you can see that except in the first and last cells in a routing, a job will always have two POLCA cards with it when it is being actively worked on in any of the intermediate cells in its routing. So the POLCA loops overlap throughout the routing except at the first and last cell.

Although this overlapping effect is simply a consequence of applying the POLCA scheduling rules to each job, it has two positive effects on the interactions between cell teams. First, this feature explicitly recognizes that each cell in the routing for a particular order is potentially a supplier as well as a customer to another cell. Therefore the POLCA loops permit each cell to allocate capacity to jobs and schedule production using information about requirements and the current workload in its customer and supplier cells. Secondly, the requirement that the downstream cell finish work on the job before sending the POLCA card back ensures that jobs with problems (e.g., quality/rework issues) are not continually pushed aside in favor of starting new jobs. If a job does get pushed aside due to a problem, that will hold up a POLCA card, which reduces the number of additional jobs that can come into the cell. So there is an incentive to finish jobs already in the cell before starting new jobs. This results in speedier resolution of problems and, therefore, reduction of MCT in the downstream cell.

Benefits Realized with POLCA Implementations

During the past few years POLCA has been implemented in many different types of manufacturing enterprises and has proved itself to be very robust in terms of both the size of the system and the type of product being made. Examples range from a small application consisting of one sheet metal fabrication cell feeding seven electrical assembly cells, to a very large application consisting of dozens of machining cells feeding each other in complex patterns in the process of making parts for big mining equipment. Also, POLCA does not have to be confined to manufacturing. Companies have included office cells and stockrooms in the POLCA system as well. Now I summarize the main benefits that have been experienced with POLCA.

- POLCA builds on the cellular organization; it builds on your existing MRP system instead of replacing it; and it builds on the teamwork and ownership. A comment from one company was that hours and hours of managers' and supervisors' time were liberated each week from the ability of the cells and teams to follow the schedule and keep on track. Indeed, in most manufacturing companies with the familiar protocol of hot jobs and rush orders, a lot of managerial time is consumed in deciding between expediting choices and reassigning resources to serve the expedited jobs. By not needing to spend all this time in "firefighting," managers can spend more time in strategic matters and in looking for ways to improve the operation, with better long-term results. The enterprise can also run with fewer layers of management, resulting in more efficient operation and lower overhead.

- POLCA cards ensure the best use of capacity; they also help to avoid congestion on the shop floor due to jobs being launched early or jobs being stacked up at bottlenecks. P&H Mining Equipment, a division of Joy Global Inc., manufactures very large custom-engineered equipment such as mining shovels, draglines, and blast hole drills, and has annual sales of over $1 billion. P&H had been implementing QRM for several years including shop floor cells and office Q-ROCs, and in 2006 it decided to connect around a dozen shop floor cells and a few other facilities such as heat treat using POLCA. During the very first year that POLCA was implemented, P&H reduced its WIP by $3 million—and this was not due to falling demand. Quite the contrary—this WIP reduction with POLCA occurred in the face of increasing production targets. Bob Mueller, factory manager at P&H, states, "POLCA has been a very good fit for our shop. Our manufacturing process is complex, and parts need to move from cell to cell, and sometimes to non-cell areas as well. POLCA keeps all of these areas working together, and the results have been solid." According to Kathy Pelto, project manager at P&H, "Kanban was simply not an effective option for us. POLCA has helped us identify many shop floor sequencing issues that went unnoticed before. It also has helped us utilize capacity in a more efficient manner. We are very pleased with the results of our POLCA implementation."

- Since POLCA cards are not linked to part numbers as in Kanban, there is no inventory proliferation when you have a large number of low-volume products. In fact since the POLCA system works under the framework of HL/MRP, when a cell gets a POLCA card that doesn't mean it has to make more parts. (This was the problem in case of the Kanban system with the low-volume axle—you made more as soon as you got the signal.) With POLCA, you work on a job only if you have a POLCA card *and* the HL/MRP system tells you that a job is needed.

- Also, since the POLCA cards are not linked to specific parts, the system works equally well for custom-engineered products. You will recall that the Kanban system can't be used when a product is custom-engineered.

- In contrast to the typical firefighting scenario where shop floor people are constantly pulled in different directions to service various hot jobs, the scheduling rules in POLCA are simple and make the job of the cell team clear. This is highlighted by the following quote from a manager at one of the first POLCA implementations: "The folks on the floor love the process. They are the ones that are really singing the praises of POLCA. Their feeling is that WIP has been reduced and that the coordination between the cells is far better."

- With the reduction in firefighting time by both managers and shop floor personnel, with less expediting, tearing down and redoing setups, and so on, one company reported a 15% increase in production capacity after implementing POLCA, with no addition of people or machines.

- POLCA helps to flag frequently occurring bottlenecks and also induces behavior to solve the problem. The absence of a POLCA card signals a downstream bottleneck and also shows which cell is causing it; if upstream cells are frequently held up by the same cell, teams will realize this and work with management to find a solution, since the bottleneck ends up impacting those teams' cells too. In the absence of such a system, bottlenecks may not be apparent to the rest of the organization, plus there is no incentive for other areas to help alleviate them.

- Note that the POLCA system resequences jobs at each step of their routing through the cells, since each cell team must go through the POLCA rules to decide which job to start next. Jobs that are behind bubble up to the top of the Dispatch List and get worked on first, but at the same time, areas of the shop that are bottlenecked get avoided and work is sent to other areas that can use it. The result of this is that over time companies experience better on-time delivery while at the same time carrying less inventory. This truly flies in the face of traditional inventory planning that says that to improve your service level to the customer you need to carry more inventory.

In conclusion, results from several years of implementing POLCA at many different types of companies demonstrate that POLCA is an effective system that brings together all the pieces of QRM strategy to ensure the successful execution of the strategy. At the same time the system is well liked by shop floor operators, planners, and schedulers, as well as management. Appendix E (on the enclosed CD) provides practical tips to assist you with designing and implementing POLCA for your situation.

TRANSFORMING YOUR PURCHASING USING TIME-BASED SUPPLY MANAGEMENT

Now that I have explained the QRM approach to material planning and control within your factory walls, I will move on to how to reorganize the planning and control of material flow from external suppliers to your factory. If you think your purchasing function has worked quite well over the years, you might well wonder why you need to change anything for QRM. To see that there is indeed a need to change your current approach, let's revisit another item from the QRM quiz, which presents a standard practice in purchasing: Since long lead time items need to be ordered in large quantities, we should negotiate quantity discounts with our suppliers (**Traditional Belief #6**).

The Response Time Spiral in Purchasing

The problem with the preceding belief is that it results in another Response Time Spiral (see Figure 4.10). To understand this spiral, let's say Becky is a buyer/planner in your purchasing department. We'll start at the top of the diagram in Figure 4.10 and follow the arrows. For a given set of parts, Becky has to work with an established supplier that has long lead

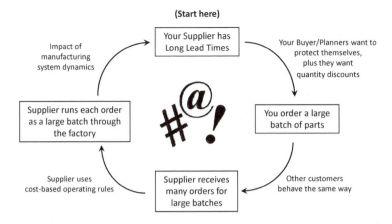

FIGURE 4.10
The Response Time Spiral for purchasing from suppliers.

times (I'll explain in the following paragraph why this is often the case). Becky wants to protect herself against running out of those parts in case of unanticipated demand changes—she would be held responsible by management if the shop floor ran out of those parts and production got held up. Since the supplier has long lead times and can't react fast enough to your demand changes, Becky plans to order a large batch of parts from the supplier—this quantity includes a sufficient safety stock of extra parts to guard against those unexpected increases in your production. At the same time, this gives Becky the leverage to negotiate a price discount with the supplier—also a plus for Becky since her annual performance review is greatly weighted by the price reductions she is able to achieve for her portfolio of purchased parts. So Becky has two incentives to order in large batches. She negotiates with the supplier, achieves an acceptable price discount for the large order, and places her order with the supplier.

Let's shift to the supplier's operation. This supplier has a number of other customers, and the buyer/planners at these other organizations face the same issues as Becky and behave in the same manner. Thus the supplier receives many orders for large batches of parts. At this point, since managers at the supplier's factory use cost-based operating rules, they assume that running large batches is a good idea as it lowers the standard cost of production for each of these orders. So they run all the orders through their shop floor in these large batch sizes. Now we know from Chapter 3 that large batches create long Flow Times through a factory. In turn, these long Flow Times require long planning lead times to be used at the supplier's factory, so the supplier's sales organization has to quote long lead times to the customer. This gets worse over time too! Since long planning lead times are in use at the supplier's factory, the Response Time Spiral for planning comes into play as I explained in Chapter 2, and the supplier's planning lead times get even longer. Now Becky has to place orders for even larger batches of parts with even more safety stock included in each order. And so on—you can see that the Response Time Spiral for purchasing has struck your operations.

Impact of Supplier with Long MCT

Why do you care if your supplier does indeed have long lead times? What if this supplier has the lowest price, excellent quality, and a stellar track record for on-time delivery? (In fact, this may be why this supplier was selected in the first place.) To answer this, let's examine the true impact of a supplier that has long lead times—or to be more precise, let's examine the impact of a supplier with a long MCT. Remember that the definition of MCT now starts with you as the customer, and includes all the times in the supply process through the critical path as explained in Chapter 1. So the MCT value will include not only the planned lead time of the supplier but also other times in the supplier's system including office times, component production, stocking points, and other factors discussed in Chapter 1.

What is then the "true cost" to you of sourcing from a supplier with a long MCT? For the sake of discussion, let's say this supplier is located in the Far East and even though this supplier's lead times include 4 to 6 weeks of shipping time and another 4 to 6 weeks of factory lead time, the supplier was selected because of its low cost along with an acceptable quality and delivery track record. Let's also say that you have a quoted price of $500 per piece for the parts from this supplier, and this price includes all the logistics costs, so this appears to be the full cost of receiving these parts at your factory. In actual fact, due to the long MCT there is the potential for you to incur the following costs in addition to the quoted price for the parts:

- High inventory costs to guard against unexpected demand changes.
- Freight costs for rush shipments if inventory runs out. These costs can mount up fast if they involve air shipments from overseas.
- The cost of unplanned engineering changes creating obsolete inventory—and not just inventory at your location, but throughout the supply chain for this supplier, potentially including parts already

shipped and in transit, and intermediate stocks and components at the supplier's factory. Plus, now that the inventory at your factory and all the inventory on its way is not usable due to the engineering change, you will need to place rush orders with high freight cost to get the parts to your factory in time to fulfill your production requirements.

- The cost due to quality problems creating obsolete inventory—all the remarks about inventory in the previous point apply here too, including the need to now place rush orders with high freight cost.
- During the long MCT, you will incur considerable costs of personnel time for communications with the supplier. The longer the MCT, the more numerous are the intermediate communications that need to take place for your purchasing staff to check with the supplier about the status of the order, whether it has been shipped, if it is in transit or in customs, and so on.
- In addition, with a long MCT there are bound to be forecast changes and schedule changes during this long period and you will incur the costs of personnel time for dealing with these with the supplier.
- The long MCT will mean reduced flexibility in your ability to respond to demand changes. Indeed over the past few years, as many organizations jumped on the bandwagon to outsource parts overseas to lower cost countries, many of them subsequently reported that they had lost significant sales opportunities due to unavailability of some long lead time components which meant that they in turn could not make the products in time to meet the sales season.
- Finally, for custom-engineered products if the components from the supplier also need to be custom-designed for each order, then the long MCT at the supplier will mean that your quoted lead times will need to be very long as well, resulting in many dysfunctional effects in your organization as well as the potential to lose sales to competitors.

Most companies greatly underestimate these additional costs. In fact, since the performance of the purchasing department is evaluated based on purchased price of parts and these additional costs are incurred after the purchasing decisions are executed, there is every incentive for purchasing staff to chase after low-cost suppliers regardless of their lead times. This is exacerbated by the fact that many of the costs mentioned simply get absorbed into overhead and don't clearly get attributed to the purchasing decisions. Studies show, however, that when carefully enumerated, these costs can increase the actual cost to the organization of using those parts by as much as 40% to 60% over the quoted price.

Deficiencies of Traditional Supply Management Metrics

Building on the preceding points, let me review the traditional approach to sourcing decisions so that you see that the significance of MCT goes beyond the effects described. The three traditional metrics used for supplier evaluation are quality, cost, and delivery. Consider a supplier with a long MCT due to inefficient operations in its organization, and consider how this supplier might fare on the three traditional metrics:

- **Quality** is measured "as delivered" to the customer. Even if the supplier has poor quality processes, through instituting multiple inspection steps the supplier can ensure that parts delivered to the customer meet a high quality standard.
- **Cost** for the supplier is not known to the customer but is inferred from the quoted price, and it is assumed that a low price means the supplier has low cost. In actual fact an inefficient supplier might simply be quoting low prices by cutting on margins and not investing in improvements.
- **Delivery** is measured as "on-time" to the customer. Even with long MCTs and unpredictable operations the supplier can achieve good delivery by holding lots of finished-goods inventory.

What do these points mean for your supply management operations? They show that the traditional supplier metrics allow your suppliers to hide their inefficiencies. This is because these metrics tell you what the supplier has done for you, but they do not tell you *how* the supplier achieved this performance. But if you are getting quality parts on time and at a low price, do you care? Yes, you absolutely should care, because one of two things will happen: either you will continue to pay for these inefficiencies in terms of the prices charged by the supplier, or the supplier will go out of business. In the first case, you are losing out on opportunities to squeeze cost out of your supply chain. As demonstrated in Chapter 1, if the supplier were to reduce its MCT, this would result not only in shorter lead times for you, but also better quality and lower cost for the supplier, and some of these benefits could be passed on to you as well. In the second case, your purchasing function typically spends a lot of time and effort in creating the relationship with each supplier and evaluating their performance to ensure that it meets your needs. Finding a new supplier to provide those parts will add significant cost to your operations and may also impact your ability to deliver your existing orders.

Use MCT as a Primary Metric for Suppliers

Instead of the traditional metrics, the key to the QRM approach of *time-based supply management* is the following. Include MCT as one of the primary metrics for suppliers. Motivate your suppliers to reduce their MCTs by implementing QRM, resulting in small-batch deliveries at lower cost, better quality, and shorter lead times (**QRM Principle #6**). Let's go into more detail on this approach. First, I need to clarify how you measure MCT for your supplier. The answer is simple: apply the definition exactly as in Chapter 1, but with your company as the "customer." Appendix A (on the enclosed CD) covers many details on applying this metric properly and you can follow the instructions there; but again, in looking at those remember that for measuring your supplier's MCT you need to start with you as the customer.

Next, I will explain the benefits of this approach. In contrast to the traditional supplier metrics described, you will find the MCT metric to have several advantages:

- **It is a better indicator of a supplier's operational effectiveness.** Think about it this way: suppose you have two suppliers making a similar product at the same price, and one has an MCT of 8 weeks while the other has an MCT of 2 weeks. Does this not tell you that the second supplier is doing something better? In fact, as discussed throughout this book, long MCTs lead to many dysfunctional effects—these will be present more so at the first supplier and much less at the second.
- **It gives you a clear evaluation of the supplier's ability to respond to changes.** This includes not just responding to changes in demand but also engineering changes or those needed because of quality problems. Observe that none of the three traditional metrics gives you any indication of this ability, and also the traditional measure of lead time does not include all the other time that might be involved in internal operations and material stocks that may need to be scrapped or reworked to implement the changes.

- **It serves as an indicator of a supplier's long-term viability.** Returning to the example of the two suppliers, one with an 8-week MCT and the other with the 2-week MCT, you can see for the same reasons discussed previously that the second supplier has a healthier operation and is more likely to be successful.

In case you are concerned about implementing this radical new metric, it might reassure you to know that you don't need to scrap the traditional three metrics—they still provide useful information about the supplier—so you can keep using them, but supplement them with the MCT metric. However, you should elevate the importance of MCT in this set of metrics because it is truly a measure of the pulse of the supplier's operation. If you have followed all the arguments in this book then you understand that in the long run the supplier's cost, quality, and delivery performance all depend on the supplier's MCT.

Encourage Your Suppliers to Reduce MCT

The preceding point leads to the next step in time-based supply management. Once you have obtained the MCT value for a supplier, you should encourage that supplier's management to reduce their MCT. QRM tells us that as the supplier's MCT is reduced, their quality and delivery will improve and they will be able to make smaller batches with quick response times, all of which will make your operation more effective as well. In addition, their cost will go down, which can result in price reductions for you as well. Keeping in mind these benefits, you can go a step further and assign some of your own staff's time to go and work with the supplier to help them in initiating QRM projects to reduce their MCT. Even though you will bear some of the costs of this support to the supplier, in the long term the benefits to your organization can be substantially more than these costs.

In order to get management at the supplier's operation to buy into the MCT reduction approach, you will most likely also have to educate key managers on the basics of QRM and deal with the traditional mind-set at the executive level of the supplier's company. Encourage supplier personnel to attend QRM training sessions, or even invest in QRM training at the supplier's location. Beyond this, note that Chapter 5 has a road map to guide you with implementing QRM at your organization; you may find that this road map also helps you tackle the supplier's organization.

Another factor that helps the implementation of MCT as a metric is that your suppliers don't see it as an invasive metric—they will not be defensive in sharing their MCT data with you. In contrast, if you asked to see a supplier's cost data, management at the supplier would be highly reluctant to share that with you since they would expect you to use that to your advantage in price negotiations with them. But that same management would be more open to looking into the time that it takes for jobs to flow through their organization and sharing that data with you since there would not be a clear way for you to use that to negotiate terms with them.

Time-Based Dual Sourcing for Overseas Suppliers

Since the QRM approach places such great emphasis on MCT as a metric, and overseas suppliers will always have a long MCT due to transportation times, does this mean that QRM theory says that you can't use distant suppliers such as low-cost suppliers in Asia? No, that is not implied by QRM; however, QRM does advocate a different decision-making process for use of distant suppliers. I will explain this process next.

For parts that you are sourcing in high volume, that have a mature design, and that have relatively predictable demand (in other words you are quite confident about your forecasts), the supplier location is irrelevant. You can source these parts from anywhere in the world since you can plan accurately for their delivery regardless of the transportation times.

For parts that are being sourced with high volume but for which the demand could be quite volatile (in other words the actual demand could be significantly different from your forecasts), you need to use a QRM strategy called *time-based dual sourcing*. Most purchasing people understand the concept of dual sourcing, which is simply to have at least two suppliers for a given component, so as not to be held hostage by a sole supplier. However, time-based dual sourcing uses this approach differently, to overcome the disadvantages caused by long MCTs. In this case you have two suppliers with different characteristics:

- You have a distant supplier that has been selected primarily for cost reasons. You negotiate with this supplier to provide enough parts for that portion of demand for which you are confident. For example, let's say that this supplier provides rear axles for tractors made by you. Suppose that for next April your sales forecast for a particular line of tractors is 200 during the month. Upon additional questioning and brainstorming, the sales group tells you that they are very confident you will ship at least 160 tractors; their best guess for the total shipments is 200; and if you have a really good month you might even ship 230. Then you should contract with your distant supplier to deliver the 160 axles needed for the minimum number of tractors expected to be shipped in April. Note that because of the location of this supplier, this number will need to be firmed up and the order placed many months in advance of April.

- As the other component of this sourcing strategy, you need to find a local supplier with short MCT who can also supply these same rear axles. You will then place orders with this supplier for the required number of axles close to the time that you need them. For example, as you approach the month of April and you have a better handle on what your actual shipments will be, you can order the axles from this supplier. For instance, if in March it is clear that the April number will be 180 tractors, then you need to order only 20 axles from this supplier (160 are coming from the other supplier). On the other hand, if sales for this tractor are suddenly taking off and in March you realize you will probably sell 225 tractors during April, then you can order 65 axles.

The local supplier will most likely have a higher price than the distant supplier. So why should you pay more by sourcing any parts from this supplier? Using the numbers from the preceding example, we can understand the strength of the time-based dual sourcing strategy. Let's say instead of using this approach, you simply sourced all the axles from the distant supplier using the best-guess forecast. This means that for April you would have ordered 200 axles. Because of the long MCT for this supplier, you cannot really change this quantity without several months of notice to the supplier. So if in April your sales are only 180 tractors, you will end up paying for 20 extra axles and carrying these in your inventory. Also, chances are your sales for future months are also lower than expected, but you have a pipeline of parts on their way from the supplier, so this excess inventory is not going to get used up soon; if anything it will continue to grow for a while. In the opposite scenario, if in April you have the potential to sell 225 tractors, you will lose the opportunity to sell 25 of them since you just won't have the axles on hand in time. Thus in both scenarios you are incurring costs or losing revenue because of your decision to use the distant supplier. This additional cost or lost revenue would be avoided by the dual-sourcing approach, even though it would add to the average sourcing cost of those components.

The preceding was an example for just one component being sourced for one line of your products. In any manufacturing enterprise, you have hundreds or thousands of components to source, and also for a large number of different products. When you add together over a period of time the potential costs or lost sales resulting from all the sourcing decisions from distant suppliers, the total monetary amounts can be substantial. These lost profits can be reduced by use of the dual-sourcing strategy.

How do you decide on the specifics of the strategy? There are essentially only two parameters to decide on for each component that is being sourced, namely, how much to source each month (or week) from the distant supplier and how much of a price premium you should be willing to pay for the local supplier. If you have the organizational time and skills to engage in what-if exercises, then the best approach is for your sales, purchasing, and planning people to brainstorm alternative forecast versus actual sales scenarios and calculate typical costs of those scenarios in order to make their decisions. However, this can be a daunting exercise as it may require a lot of effort and skills in performing the what-ifs. An easier alternative is to use the following simple rules of thumb based on costs I have observed at many QRM companies.

First, for a given product, and for each forecast period (e.g., week or month) get your salespeople to commit to a minimum sales target that they are "very confident" they can achieve—note that this is not the same as a forecast, which attempts to predict the typical sales; this is the absolute least amount that they think will be sold. Order this quantity from the distant supplier for delivery in each period. Second, in terms of the local supplier with short MCT, be willing to pay a price premium of up to 60% (over the distant supplier's price) in selecting such a supplier. Over time the overall benefits to your enterprise of using this time-based dual-sourcing approach will exceed the incremental costs of the parts sourced from the more expensive local supplier.

Strategies for Low-Volume Parts

For low-volume or custom-engineered parts, you should question the need to search for overseas sources at all. For low-volume parts, when you consider all the potential additional costs due to the long MCT plus the overhead of finding the low-cost supplier with the right abilities and setting up the relationship, it's just not worth it. For customized parts, you cannot even try to mitigate the long MCT by carrying inventory. Hence the overseas supplier will add a significant amount of time to your MCT and magnify the dysfunctional effects in your organization. In addition, this will require you to quote very long lead times to your customers and potentially lose sales as well. Thus for both low-volume and custom-engineered parts, it is unlikely that the use of low-cost overseas suppliers would be beneficial. You are better off developing a relationship with local suppliers and working with them to reduce their MCTs with many benefits to you over time.

For low-volume or custom-engineered parts, one additional time-based supply management strategy is to reserve supplier capacity instead of booking specific orders for parts. Suppose you expect to order 100 castings a month from a supplier, to be used for machining custom-engineered housings, but you don't know the specifications of the castings ahead of time. If you wait till the specifications have been engineered and then place the order, you may have to wait behind a lot of other customer orders at the foundry and experience long delivery times. However, if you negotiate a contract with a supplier that guarantees you a specific amount of capacity each week, then as soon as you know your part specifications you can place the order and be slotted into the schedule right away. This approach is the same as the "time-slicing" method, which can be used for internal shared resources and is described in Appendix C (see the enclosed CD). Essentially you are purchasing slices of time at the supplier's operation to support your operation. Of course there is a trade-off here—if you reserve capacity but don't use it, you may have to pay the supplier an agreed-upon amount anyway—but this should be countered by the benefits obtained most of the other times when you get your parts quickly and this supports your manufacturing and sales strategies better.

Supplement Time-Based Strategies with Other Modern Practices

The preceding are the key components of the QRM approach to supply management. However, these time-based supply management methods do not have to be implemented in isolation, nor do other methods have to be discarded. These QRM techniques can be supplemented with other proven modern practices that may already be in use at your organization. Examples of these are: vendor-managed inventory (VMI) and point-of-use (POU) inventory for low-cost and commonly used components such as bolts, brackets, screws, washers, and the like; sharing your forecasts and schedules with your suppliers so they can support your operation better; and use of electronic data interchange (EDI) or other newer Web-based interfaces.

Train Your Supply Management Personnel and Rethink Performance Metrics

Finally, to ensure that your time-based supply management strategy is successfully executed, don't forget to invest in educating your supply management staff. Many of them have years of experience working with the traditional purchasing mind-set of ordering large batches and asking for quantity discounts, or chasing price reductions wherever possible. Start by educating them in basic principles of QRM, followed by the Response Time Spiral for purchasing so that they understand why the traditional approach might be dysfunctional in the context of your new QRM strategy. Help them see that reducing their suppliers' MCTs will also reduce the time they spend in firefighting and give them more time for strategic activities including supplier development—this will also increase their buy-in to the QRM approach. Then work together with them on a road map for transitioning the purchasing operations to meet the new goals.

As part of this road map you will have to rethink performance measures for purchasing personnel as well. In particular, instead of just evaluating them based on price reductions achieved with their suppliers, in their annual performance review you could also include the MCT reductions achieved by their suppliers (measured by their suppliers' QRM Numbers). This will give your purchasing staff an incentive to work with suppliers to reduce their MCTs.

Customer Strategies to Support Your QRM Program

Before concluding this section on time-based supply management, I'd like to point out that your supply chain doesn't end when material arrives at your factory—it ends when material arrives at your customer! So you also need to reexamine the interactions with your customer—in fact your organizational policies might be creating a spiral of longer and longer lead times. Consider a traditional belief propagated by the sales organization which was stated in the QRM quiz: We should encourage our customers to buy our products in large quantities by offering price breaks and quantity discounts (**Traditional Belief #7**).

By this point in the book you have seen enough examples of the dysfunctional effects of large batches to know where this is going, but I'll summarize the main point again. The incentives for your sales force motivate them to offer quantity discounts in an attempt to garner larger orders. This is reinforced by your traditional costing system, which makes you think you these larger jobs will cost less. The large batches ordered by many customers then degrade your company's delivery performance. This further encourages the customers to order ahead with larger quantities. To understand this last statement, a simple analogy helps drive home the point. Earlier in this chapter I discussed the Response Time Spiral that results from your purchasing staff placing orders for large batches at your suppliers. Now switch hats for a moment and consider that in the customers' eyes, you are the supplier; think of the decision making by the customer's purchasing staff as explained earlier, and you'll see why they decide to order even larger batches. Thus the interplay between the customers' policies and your internal policies results in a similar spiral between you and your customer. Instead, the QRM approach is as follows: Make your customers aware of your QRM program, and work with them to transition to a schedule of smaller batch deliveries at reasonable prices (**QRM Principle #7**).

The first point to note is that your customers may not necessarily be thrilled about the ability to order smaller batches. Not only will they be concerned about the increased price for these smaller batches, but possibly more significantly, their purchasing staff may not trust your ability to deliver in a short lead time—think of your past track record and why their purchasing staff is ordering large batches "just to be safe" as explained in Figure 4.10. Thus a stepwise transition might be needed to undo the spiral effect.

Let's take a specific customer as an example. You start implementing your QRM program and somewhat reduce your lead times for this customer's parts. As the customer observes that you are consistently achieving these shorter lead times, the purchasing staff feel a bit more secure about working with a shorter planning horizon for those parts, and place orders for smaller batches. These smaller batches further enhance your ability to reduce your lead times to this customer, and so on. It is also easy to modify your pricing approach so that both your sales staff and your customer remain happy with the situation of smaller batches. Instead of offering quantity discounts for orders placed at one time, offer a comparable discount for the total quantity ordered over a time period, say over a year. But how do you execute this strategy and price your products when you don't know at the beginning of the year what the total order quantity will be for this customer? The answer to this is simple too. Pick a smaller time period (e.g., a quarter) and every quarter calculate a discount and apply it to the next quarter's billing. The discounts will get bigger as the year goes on, to take into account the cumulative quantity ordered. This will also make your customer feel happier over the year.

The story doesn't stop here. As your MCT for these parts falls, we know that your quality will improve and your costs will go down, so you can offer even more competitive pricing to your customer. Beyond that, the customer's planning staff will start to realize that they need to carry less inventory of your products, to plan less far ahead, and to have fewer expediting and other overhead activities involved in interactions with you. All of this will strengthen your position with this customer.

Get Your Sales Force to Exploit Your QRM Capabilities

Your salespeople can also play a proactive rather than a passive role in this process. When stating the QRM principle, I mentioned making your customer aware of your QRM program. Your sales force should preview some of these expected results with your customers early on, so they see the benefits of using you as a supplier.

Moving beyond this, as your track record and capabilities for quick response improve, your salespeople should look for opportunities to exploit this to increase your market share. For instance, original equipment manufacturers (OEMs) typically don't do a good job of exploiting their own aftermarket business. This is because for many OEMs that make specialized equipment in lower volumes, lead time and fill rate performances of their parts suppliers can be notoriously poor—lead times of 6 months or more, and complete order fill rates of 50% or less. Since the OEMs rely on these suppliers for their parts, many OEMs do not reliably serve their aftermarket. If your products fit the bill for any of these OEMs, then get your salespeople to sell your capability to them with the proposition that having you as a supplier will enable them to increase their aftermarket share. This is just one example; encourage your people in marketing and sales to find other similar opportunities to take advantage of your quick response capability.

TIME-BASED MIND-SET FOR NEW-PRODUCT INTRODUCTION

With today's fast-paced changes in technology, markets, and customer preferences, new products are the lifeblood of a manufacturing business. Indeed, the most successful companies typically get 50% or more of their sales from products introduced within the previous 5 years. There is a lot of literature about new-product development, and many proven techniques already abound such as concurrent engineering and quality function deployment (QFD), so I will not attempt to duplicate those ideas here. Instead, I will focus on how management can extend QRM principles to support rapid new-product introduction (NPI). The key once again is to transform your NPI process and decision making using time-based thinking instead of cost-based thinking.

Benefits of Rapid New-Product Introduction

The first step in this transformation is for management to truly appreciate the strategic advantages of rapid NPI. Although all managers intuitively relate to the benefits of speed to market, they typically underestimate the rewards that can be obtained with consistently fast introduction of new products. Figure 4.11 compares a QRM company that has a 2-year "concept to customer" cycle with that of a competitor that has a 4-year cycle. The figure helps to illustrate two benefits of rapid NPI. The first benefit is obvious to most people—that the QRM company introduces the product earlier and has 2 years during which it can capture market share. The second benefit is often overlooked.

The lowest arrow in the figure shows that while the competitor starts its NPI process in 2010 and introduces its product in 2014, with a shorter NPI cycle the QRM company can start its product development in 2012 and still bring its product to market in 2014. What does this mean? With the high rate of change in today's world as I mentioned earlier, the QRM company's rapid process will provide it with several advantages:

- In a typical NPI process, you have to lock into your choice of technologies within the first 20% of your time window. Thus the competitor's product would be based on technology available in 2010 while the QRM company's product could use technology that becomes

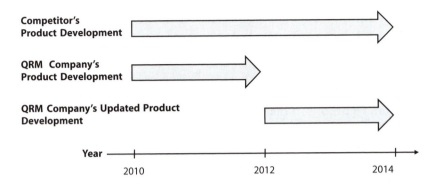

FIGURE 4.11
Strategic advantages of rapid new-product introduction.

available in 2012. In today's world, particularly with the rate of change in electronics and materials, 2 years could make a huge difference. The QRM company's design team could take advantage of more powerful and cheaper electronic components, new controls, new composites and other materials, and so on. Thus their product would hit the market with significantly better functionality than the competitor's product, which would look archaic in comparison.

- The manufacturing processes used by the QRM company for the new product could also be based on the latest technologies such as new laser machining methods, rapid prototyping, or nanofabrication. This might enable cheaper production, better quality products or both. Not only that, but during the design phase the engineers could take advantage of these new processing technologies to push the limits of their design and increase the functional capability of the product.

- The competitor's marketing team would have to lock into product functionality decisions 4 years prior to the product launch, while the QRM company's team would need to do this only 2 years prior to launch. Again, with the frequent changes in markets and customer preferences today, this gives the QRM company a higher chance of targeting the right markets and customers.

- The preceding point can have a huge leverage effect; in fact another Response Time Spiral comes into play here. When the NPI cycle is long, during the development there can be a significant shift in the marketplace, causing the marketing staff to rethink their choice of product features and options. This requires redesign and possibly reevaluation of prototypes, thereby drawing out the development process. In turn, during the longer development process, marketing may again insist that more changes are needed; and so the spiral continues. In contrast, with a rapid NPI process, the product can be introduced before significant market shifts occur. Moreover, as seen from Figure 4.11, if the market is indeed shifting, the QRM company will have a chance to get its first version out into the market and still carry out a second full development cycle to meet with the new market needs in the same time that the competitor introduces the product based on its original market projections.

Finally, a shorter NPI process has another leveraging effect too. The organization can engage in more new-product introduction cycles as seen in the previous point, but in addition it has fewer active projects at any time. With long NPI cycles, each project stays in the system longer and so there are a lot of active projects. This has another dysfunctional effect, which is that resources such as engineers are pulled in different directions trying to support multiple projects and cannot work efficiently on any one of them, further lengthening the project times. Just like the hot-job situation on the shop floor, this effect too can be exacerbated as management decides that a particular project has fallen behind and might have a critical impact on sales. So the development team gets a "drop everything" order from management in order to focus on this one project. Of course this means that the other projects now fall behind. Another Response Time Spiral comes into play. On the other hand, with a rapid NPI process, teams can focus on getting each project out efficiently and then move on to the next one.

So what do all these points add up to? They mean that in the NPI process too, time has a very high value—or to paraphrase the statement I made at the beginning of this book, time in the NPI process is also a lot more money than most managers realize. Conversely, managers that do realize this can transform their decision making to better support rapid NPI. As you have seen throughout this book, there is typically a lack of measurement of elapsed time in various organizational processes, and the NPI process is no different. The absence of proper measurements also means that management is unaware of the magnitude of problems that may be occurring. Thus you should begin by applying the MCT metric to the NPI process so that you start to gather data on your current NPI performance. As I explained in Chapter 1, for consistency of the name of the metric throughout the organization, we still call it MCT, but you can clarify its application to NPI by using phrases such as "our MCT for NPI is 14 months" or "the NPI MCT is 14 months." Note however that the starting point of the NPI MCT measurement should be from the first time that the initial concept is formally aired by the sales or R&D organization, and the ending point should be when the first product is shipped to an actual customer. Between these points you should be sure to map out all the ancillary processes that impact this NPI process. To help you understand what I mean by this, I will give you instances of these ancillary processes in the following section.

Rethinking Cost-Based Decisions for New-Product Introduction

After becoming more aware of the impact of MCT for your NPI process, you then need to rethink conventional cost-based decisions in terms of their impact on this NPI MCT. I will illustrate this with a few examples.

Implement a New Purchasing Paradigm for Prototype Construction

The construction and testing of prototypes is a significant part of the product development process. The manufacture of these prototypes often requires purchasing of new materials or parts that are not already in the organization. This purchasing process, however, usually goes through the same channels as purchasing for production parts. This means that the standard processes are applied, such as getting competitive quotes from vendors, looking for the lowest cost vendor, and not giving priority to lead times. The prototype completion time is then hostage to the longest lead time component. (The MCT metric along with MCT Mapping helps to highlight such situations. See Appendix A on the enclosed CD for examples.) It turns out, however, that this problematic lead time can be significantly impacted with just a small increase in purchasing cost, as the following case study shows.

A manufacturer of electronic controls for complex electrical systems had long prototype production times, primarily due to long procurement times for components. An analysis of the component lead times showed that only a few of the components were responsible for the long procurement times. If the company would have been willing to pay a 10% to 15% price premium on each of these components, it could have found short-lead-time suppliers for all of them. Further analysis showed an amazing insight—resourcing of these components would add only 3% to the total cost of the NPI project, yet would reduce the total lead time for making prototypes from weeks to a few days. The reason the cost increment was so small was that, first, the cost of all purchased components was only a small part of the total NPI project cost, which included costs of engineering, testing, market surveys, process development, and so on, and second, only a few key components needed to be resourced. However, because the company was stuck in the traditional purchasing paradigms of looking for the most economical suppliers, no one had conducted this analysis.

The moral of the case study is the following QRM approach. In the context of an NPI project, rethink your traditional decision-making paradigms: look at decisions that influence the major drivers of MCT for the NPI project and for each of them ask yourself how you would rethink these decisions to achieve the primary goal of reducing the total NPI MCT. The best approach to doing this is to brainstorm ideas with the cross-functional team that is involved in the whole NPI project. As one example, for the case study just described, a possible solution would be to have a separate purchasing paradigm for prototyping where the buyer would be given a budgeted amount of discretionary spending that could be used to reduce component lead times without requiring the usual competitive quoting from suppliers. The buyer could even have a few trusted suppliers with blanket purchase orders already in place to further reduce the purchasing formalities and time.

Identify Long-Lead-Time Components Ahead of Time

The preceding approach can be supported by various proactive organizational initiatives. For instance, engineering and purchasing could get together and generate a list of long-lead-time components. Then, during the NPI project, designers could either try to avoid using these components, or else alert the buyers early in the project to start procuring them even while the design is in a preliminary phase. Admittedly, there might be instances where the component is no longer required as the design progresses, but again, from the previous example, a small cost overrun in component purchasing is but a fraction of the cost of the total project, while the returns due to shorter lead times can be huge. Another option, where the supplier is known but the details of the component are not yet clear, is to reserve capacity at the supplier for the date when the design will be ready, so that the supplier can be prepared and have the capacity to turn the order around quickly. These are but a few examples; as your teams engage in NPI projects, they should use each project experience as a means to develop other such tools to help reduce your NPI MCT. Over time, the set of these tools will make your organization increasingly more effective in rapidly introducing new products.

It's not just management that needs to rethink its decision-making paradigms. The typical modern approach to NPI is to form cross-functional teams that engage in concurrent engineering—these teams should be educated in QRM principles and thinking, and should start using MCT as an important criterion during team sessions. For instance, they could rethink entire development procedures to see if processes that are currently done sequentially could be done in parallel instead. These teams too will need to shift away from the mind-set of cost-based thinking and challenge the conventional decision trade-offs using time as a decision driver instead.

Use Product Enrichment Strategy

This is another example to show how teams can rethink traditional paradigms. Typically when a new product line is being introduced, marketing looks at various options in the new product, stratified at different cost levels. While the multitude of options might be a good idea in terms of finding the right combination of features and costs to appeal to an individual customer, the resulting plethora of designs, components, prototypes, and testing processes can add major delays to a project. An alternative is to use the strategy of product enrichment. The idea is to combine several features into an enhanced product, but to still offer it at the price level of some of the simpler features. While this may appear to be a profit-losing proposition, that is not the case. The reduction in NPI time, combined with the ease of purchasing components and producing a lower number of products, will significantly reduce all the overhead costs associated with this product line. In addition, customers will be amazed at all the functionalities they can get for what seems to be a very competitive cost, so sales for this product line could also be much higher than in the case of multiple stratified options.

The combined impact of all these changes can be substantial. By training its NPI teams in QRM and implementing time-based approaches, a manufacturer of sophisticated electromechanical medical instruments reduced its average NPI time from 2½ years to less than 6 months.

SUMMARY AND NEXT STEPS

In this chapter I have shown you how to extend QRM strategy to your whole enterprise. In so doing I have repeatedly talked about replacing cost-based decisions with time-based decisions and I'm sure you've been wondering how you could justify such decisions rationally. You are probably also a bit overwhelmed by the broad scope of QRM and are wondering whether you can start in one area or need to tackle the whole enterprise. Both these issues are discussed in the next chapter, where I give you a stepwise plan for implementing QRM along with pointers to help you with accounting and cost justification issues.

5

A Road Map for QRM Implementation

Now that you have seen the power of time and are convinced that you need to implement the QRM principles in order to reduce time throughout your organization, how and where do you start? In this chapter I will give you a tried-and-tested road map for implementation of QRM—this road map is based on my participation in hundreds of QRM projects in many types of companies and extracting the key elements that led to the most successes.

The first step toward implementing QRM is creating the QRM mind-set, starting with top management. You have seen throughout this book how the time-based mind-set differs—often radically—from traditional management paradigms. To begin with, it is important that your management embarks on the QRM journey for the right reasons. I have occasionally had to deal with the following mistaken impression, which you saw in the QRM quiz: The reason for implementing QRM is so that we can charge our customers more for rush jobs (**Traditional Belief #9**).

Although customers may pay more for speedy delivery, this should not be the reason for engaging in QRM. While it may appear to be a good short-term result of better response, it is risky since charging more might destroy some goodwill with your customers. Worse yet, it may even motivate them to look for alternative suppliers, so you will be helping your competition get your customers! Instead, the reason for embarking on the QRM journey is that it leads to a truly productive company with a more secure future: Shorter lead times, higher quality, and competitive prices (as a consequence of lower costs). The results are highly satisfied customers and growing market share (**QRM Principle #9**).

To summarize what you have seen throughout this book, searching for ways of squeezing time out of your whole enterprise provides numerous benefits and tremendous competitive advantage. To ensure that you have at your fingertips the main advantages of implementing QRM, I have created a quick reference to the key benefits.

Increased revenues through:

- Increased sales and market share as a result of your shorter lead times, higher quality, and lower prices compared to the competition
- Ability to create new market niches through rapid new-product introductions and to be the only supplier for those niches as the competition does not have a comparable product developed yet
- Power to change the paradigm in your industry—deliver customized products in the same lead time as your competition supplies a standard product; huge potential for taking market share away from other players

Reduced costs through:

- Reduction of systemwide costs caused by long MCT (see Chapter 1 for an extensive list of these costs); in particular, significant reduction in overhead costs
- Lower material costs through time-based supply management strategies
- Higher productivity in both shop floor and office operations, and hence lower direct and indirect personnel costs per unit of sales

Superior organization through:

- Improved integration of processes; the use of FTMSs to separate and then streamline flows, along with the use of QRM Cells, team ownership, HL/MRP and POLCA to coordinate flow results in smooth operations.
- Better work environment. Teamwork and ownership result in higher morale and a highly motivated workforce on the shop floor as well as in the office.

Satisfied customers through:

- Quick response at every stage of customer interaction. This creates favorable impressions with customers (e.g., very fast response to quote requests astounds customers and increases the chances of securing the order).

- Ability to supply high variety of options or even customized product without requiring extra lead time. This will amaze customers— if they had not anticipated their need for this item and would have been in trouble, they will note your capability and reward you with more business!

QRM is the comprehensive strategy that provides you with detailed enterprise-wide principles, all with a single-minded focus on squeezing out time. By implementing QRM, you are making your company highly successful and securing its future. While Lean Manufacturing methods have put a lot of emphasis on elimination of waste, certain types of waste caused by long lead times are ignored in those approaches. With its broader definition of waste, QRM can create an even leaner enterprise. When combined with the other competitive benefits of short response times, this ensures that your company will remain a formidable competitor for years to come.

As you look at the preceding list of benefits, some of the points may be obvious, such as increasing market share or customer satisfaction through quick response. But you may be nervous about actually realizing some of the other benefits. If you implement the time-based thinking, and in so doing you go against many traditional beliefs and even increase your standard costs, can you be really sure that you will see improved quality or lower costs? After witnessing hundreds of QRM implementations for over a decade, the evidence is clear: implementing QRM does indeed result in all these benefits. I have given you a few examples already; for instance Chapter 1 shows you the impact of QRM on cost, quality, and on-time delivery. Some numbers have been even more impressive than those. As one example, a study of twelve projects cutting across many types and sizes of companies showed that on average, implementing QRM resulted in a 25% reduction in cost for the products involved. Another finding from this study was that over half these companies were able to achieve 80% or greater reduction in MCT for those products, showing that it is not unusual to achieve such high reductions if you embark on a QRM program.

"POWER OF SIX" RULE FOR COST IMPACT OF QRM

Going beyond the anecdotal data, I have developed a simple rule of thumb to help management estimate the impact of a QRM project. (This rule was developed along with Francisco Tubino at the Center for Quick Response Manufacturing.) The rule was derived from data from a small set of QRM projects several years ago, but since then it has been applied to a large number of other projects and proved to be quite robust in its predictions. Despite the fact that in implementing QRM we try to transition to time-based thinking, management is naturally still concerned with the bottom-line impact on costs, so this rule helps address this concern. The aim of the rule is not to provide an exact number, but rather to provide a ballpark estimate to guide managers in their decision making during QRM implementation.

To explain this rule, I will define two simple ratios. One is the MCT Ratio, which I will denote by *MR,* and it is the ratio of the "after" and "before" MCT values. The other, similarly, is the Cost Ratio, *CR* for the "after" and "before" costs. More precisely,

$$MCT\ Ratio = MR = \frac{Expected\ MCT\ After\ Implementing\ QRM}{Current\ MCT}$$

$$Cost\ Ratio = CR = \frac{Expected\ Cost\ After\ Implementing\ QRM}{Current\ Cost}$$

Here, "Current Cost" denotes the unit cost of the products in the FTMS that are the target of the QRM project, and "Expected Cost After Implementing QRM" is the value that is expected after overhead reductions and other improvements have been accounted for in the unit cost. With these two ratios defined, I can state the rule. I will do so in words first, as it is simple, but then also provide the equation. I'll start with the situation where management wants to achieve a certain cost reduction target to beat the prevailing market price, and due to the nature of its low-volume or custom products it has decided to use QRM as its driving strategy. So management wants to know, in order to achieve this cost reduction target, what reduction in MCT would have to be achieved?

The answer is simple. The Power of Six Rule states that if you raise the target cost ratio to the sixth power, you get the target MCT ratio. Using the preceding notation, this can be written:

$$MR = (CR)^6$$

Let's see how this might be used in practice. Suppose—based on financial goals or on a competitive analysis—management decides that its cost reduction target is 15%. In other words, looking at these definitions, this means that *CR* = 0.85. Now raise 0.85 to the sixth power (with a calculator or spreadsheet this is easily done), which results in the value of 0.38. This means that the MCT achieved should be 38% of the current MCT, a 62% reduction. Keeping in mind that this is a rough rule of thumb, what this means is that the QRM project team should target an MCT reduction of around 60%. So the Power of Six Rule has helped to provide a concrete target for the team's improvement efforts. Instead of just pulling a number out of the air for the goal, it can be based on a rational argument.

Now let's do this in reverse. Suppose a QRM project team sees the potential to reduce MCT significantly and needs to get management buy-in to invest in the project. It would be helpful if the team could predict the cost reduction that would result from the project. So let's see how the Power of Six Rule can help. Suppose it is estimated that the QRM project could reduce MCT by around 60%. In this case we know the MCT ratio and we need to find the cost ratio, so we reverse the preceding formula. The cost ratio is given by raising the MCT ratio to the one-sixth power. In mathematical terms, by reversing this formula, we get:

$$CR = (MR)^{1/6}$$

Now let's use this formula to get the answer that the team needs. Since MCT will be reduced by 60%, the new MCT will be 40% of the current value, so *MR* = 0.4. Putting this value in the preceding formula and using a calculator or spreadsheet to raise 0.4 to the one-sixth power, we get the value *CR* = 0.86. This means that the cost after implementing the QRM project will be 86% of the current cost. In other words, we can expect a cost reduction of around 14%. (Since I have been rounding off the values, this is reasonably consistent with the 15% in the previous example.) Now the team can use this 14% value to help with cost justification of the investments for the project.

I should emphasize again that the Power of Six Rule is not intended to give exact answers, but only to provide guidelines for decision making. Nevertheless, it is better to have a rational way to set goals, or to get an estimate of what can be accomplished, rather than proceeding with arbitrary numbers. In this regard the Power of Six Rule has proven helpful to management and QRM teams alike.

MIND-SET FIRST, TECHNOLOGY LATER

By its very nature, the phrase "quick response manufacturing" conjures up a picture of sophisticated computer-aided design and automated manufacturing technology all linked together to make products quickly. Thus another misconception I have encountered is this: Implementing QRM will require large investments in technology (**Traditional Belief #10**).

It is true that new technologies such as rapid prototyping, CAD/CAM, robotics, and automation offer great opportunities for time reduction in various processing steps. Although implementing such technologies may eventually be important, there are several steps that precede this effort. From the discussion in Chapter 1, processing time is only a small fraction of your total MCT, and 95% or more of your MCT is the "white space" shown in Figure 1.3 (see Chapter 1), where no work is being done on a job. As you have also seen from preceding chapters, this white space is the result of numerous traditional policies that have been in use for decades. As a result of the long-standing implementation of these policies, not only management but also employees are convinced that these policies need to be enforced.

To combat this situation, education must be a company's first step, or else other efforts will fail. In particular, the mind-set of all employees, from the shop floor to the boardroom, from desk workers to senior managers, must be realigned to time-based thinking. Hence, to replace the traditional belief, consider the following: The biggest obstacle to QRM is not technology, but "mind-set" (**QRM Principle #10**). Management must recognize this and combat it through training for management and employees alike. Next, companies should engage in low-cost or no-cost QRM projects, leaving expensive technological solutions for a later stage.

Since QRM challenges so many of the traditional management paradigms, there will be skeptics throughout the organization, so I have found that it is better if you prove out the concepts with a couple of low-cost projects first. Examples of projects that may not require large investments are: a Q-ROC for a segment of office operations; a small QRM Cell on the shop floor that doesn't need new machines or expensive re-layout of machines, cross-training of cell team members, and reduction of batch sizes within the cell. As these projects start to show results, not only in terms of MCT but also in terms of employee enthusiasm, you will win over the skeptics and be able to propose projects that require larger investments. The case study about NOV-Orange described at the end of Chapter 2 shows just such a progression that took place in their organization with increasing investments and increasingly greater returns from QRM.

An example of beginning the QRM journey with an office project is provided by Omnipress, a Madison, Wisconsin–based printing company. Omnipress specializes in conference and meeting materials such as printed books and CDs.

In 2004, management at Omnipress decided it was time for a change. "We became really good at dropping everything to get one hot job out of the door, but it totally impacted the rest of our production flow," says David McKnight, CEO of Omnipress. "We wanted to find a way to change our production flow to finish every job faster while eliminating the growing costs from overtime and frequent rework."

Omnipress decided to implement QRM because of QRM's ability to handle custom jobs. "This focus was very important because for us, every job is a custom job," says Tracy Gundert, vice president of operations.

Omnipress started its QRM journey with the growing market for conference publications delivered on CDs. During the spring of 2004, the company worked with the Center for Quick Response Manufacturing to analyze its CD operations and develop a QRM implementation plan. Based on this, in the summer of 2004 the company reorganized its CD work flow into a Q-ROC, combining all CD-related operations into the Q-ROC team.

The results were impressive: within months, the company slashed the lead time for a conference CD by 70%. As a result of this positive experience, David McKnight and Tracy Gundert decided to reorganize the rest of the company, including office and shop floor operations.

However, there was some skepticism from employees, both in the office and in the printing operations. To help create the right mind-set, Omnipress's management decided to conduct QRM training for the whole organization. Every employee was required to attend a one-day training session in December 2004. Following this, in January 2005 the company reorganized all its operations—both office and shop floor—into cells along QRM lines.

The results again were impressive. Within just a few months the lead time to finish a print or digital job was, on average, cut by half. Before the reorganization, a bound book published via the offset printing process took almost 19 days from start to finish. Now, it is done in 10 days, and that number continues to fall. Implementation of QRM transformed the company from a fragmented operation to an agile competitor in a challenging market. "Our organization is more in a state of openness towards change. We continue to challenge ourselves to do better," states Tracy Gundert. Omnipress can now serve customers better and faster—a huge advantage in the competitive media and printing industry.

In order to support the mind-set change from cost-based to time-based thinking, you will also need to rethink your performance measures. In preceding chapters I showed you that traditional approaches based on measures of utilization, efficiency, purchasing cost, and other traditional metrics result in Response Time Spirals with increasing lead time and other dysfunctional behavior. While management will always need to have some cost-based measures for its fiduciary responsibility to shareholders as well as to satisfy tax codes, employees should be motivated by time-based measures. In particular, the QRM Number should be elevated to a primary metric for teams and projects. In the sections "Use Accounting Strategies to Support QRM" and "Switch to Time-Based Cost Justification," I also show you a few simple ways to adjust your accounting and project justification approaches to make them more supportive of QRM efforts.

EMBARKING ON YOUR QRM JOURNEY

The four core principles of QRM provide the ideal framework for the steps you need to take in order to embark on your QRM journey.

Step 1: Highlight the Power of Time for Your Organization

Create awareness of the impact of time (MCT) on your operations.

- Engage in basic QRM training for a team of management and employees so that this team understands the main concepts of QRM.
- Create an initial list of the wastes due to long MCT in your organization and put some rough dollar numbers on these items.

Use this list and the dollar numbers to motivate the formation of a high-level QRM Steering Committee charged with implementing QRM in your organization. The Steering Committee will not conduct the QRM projects but will oversee their progress. It should have enough clout to secure funding, and when needed, cut through organizational red tape and change long-standing policies.

- Appoint a QRM Champion—an experienced employee with sound QRM training and a strong believer in QRM. The QRM Champion will be more involved in the day-to-day support, coaching, and facilitation of project teams and will keep projects moving. The Champion is also a member of the Steering Committee and provides a communication link between the committee and the projects.
- The Steering Committee gets initial measures of MCT for some key products, in particular, the "white space." Rough analysis is good enough at this stage.
- Based on this analysis, the Steering Committee picks a set of products or an area as the target of the first QRM project.

Step 2: Create the Right Organizational Structure

First form a cross-functional Planning Team to study this project. This team includes people from key functional areas that have the expertise to brainstorm new processes or procedures related to the area of the project (see the NOV case study in Chapter 2 for an example of such a team).

- Train all members of the Planning Team on the basics of QRM.
- The Planning Team gets better measures of MCT for the project area and uses this along with analysis of product volumes, strategic needs, and other factors to home in on the FTMS for the QRM project.
- The Planning Team comes up with plans for a QRM Cell (or cells) for this FTMS. In the process, the team members use their knowledge of QRM principles to brainstorm alternative processes and procedures that would result in better cell integrity and shorter MCT. Hence, Planning Team members should have a good grasp of QRM principles as well as how to engage in time-based thinking (also see Appendix C on the enclosed CD).
- With the support and expertise of the QRM Champion, the Planning Team presents its recommendations to management along with a cost-benefit analysis in order to get approval for implementation. (See the following section for a time-based project justification process.)

Form the Implementation Team for the project. This team includes all the people who will be in the cells plus some key support people from the Planning Team who may have to help with the implementation.

- Train the Implementation Team in QRM principles. Also bring in experts who can help with team-building training and team processes. Form the physical cells by moving equipment or people as needed.
- Launch the cells. Give the teams ownership. Encourage and support cross-training within the cells.
- After the launch, ensure that the Implementation Team continues to get advice and direction from the QRM Champion and strong support from the Steering Committee to overcome organizational obstacles and to change long-standing policies that might be hindering the cell's performance.
- Measure MCT and implement the QRM Number as the key performance metric for the cells.

Step 3: Understand and Exploit System Dynamics

Reexamine policies on utilization and batch sizing. More specifically:

- Plan the loading of cells to maintain spare capacity.
- Encourage the cell teams to engage in a program of batch size reduction.
- If either of the above results in bottlenecks, work with the teams to alleviate these bottlenecks using the suggestions in Chapter 3.

Step 4: Build Your Enterprise-Wide, Unified Strategy

Evaluate the results of the QRM project. Recognize the teams and celebrate and publicize their successes throughout the organization.

- Build on the enthusiasm of the first set of teams. Engage in QRM training for a broader population in the company.
- Encourage employees to suggest additional FTMSs for the next set of QRM projects. Appoint additional QRM Champions if needed.
- Implement QRM in these areas using the steps outlined above.
- As more cells are formed, consider whether it is time to restructure your MRP system and also implement POLCA to coordinate flows between cells.

Extend your efforts beyond the shop floor:

- For best results, make sure that your QRM projects start to span across office operations, the shop floor, and your supply chain.
- To support these efforts, expand your MCT measurements to cover broader sections of your enterprise and supply chain. Publish QRM Numbers not only for cells but for these broader segments as well to encourage not just local but also enterprise-wide improvements.

Embedded in the preceding steps is a unique organizational structure to support your QRM implementation. Other management techniques typically suggest forming a team to conduct an improvement project. However, after many years of engaging in QRM projects I have come up with a more effective structure, which consists of four different entities identified in the preceding steps. First is the high-level QRM Steering Committee to drive QRM implementation through the right management commitment. Along with this is the QRM Champion, an experienced individual to support and facilitate the project teams on a day-to-day basis, and also provide the link between the project teams and the Steering Committee. Next is the Planning Team for each project, followed by the Implementation Team for the same project. From the details of the preceding steps you can understand the different roles of these four entities. You can also appreciate that one team could not effectively accomplish all these tasks and see the benefit of the structure I suggest. As you roll out more QRM projects, you might decide to appoint more QRM Champions and assign sets of projects or areas of the company to each champion.

SWITCH TO TIME-BASED COST JUSTIFICATION OF QRM PROJECTS

Throughout this book I have emphasized the need to shift from cost-based thinking to time-based thinking. Yet at the end of the day, as responsible management, you need to be confident that your QRM projects will provide sufficiently strong financial returns that meet or exceed your strategic goals. But if you make decisions based on time, as I have advocated, how can you connect those to specific financial goals so that you know how much to invest? Fortunately there is a rational way to do this, and this method also satisfies traditional financial standards so there should be no major objection from your financial personnel.

I call this approach time-based cost justification, and I will explain how it works with an example. Suppose your salespeople feel that you could capture significant market share for a line of customized products if you could reduce your customer response time significantly and also reduce the product price marginally. So you establish a strategic initiative to go after this opportunity. Based on preliminary analysis of MCT for this product line, as well as the required market lead time that your salespeople need you to achieve, you ascertain that to succeed in capturing the market share you need to bring the current MCT down from 13 weeks to 3 weeks. This initial analysis assumes that you will undertake QRM projects in various areas for this product line, including the office, shop floor, and supply chain. Clearly the next set of questions is: How much money should you be willing to invest in doing this, and what possible QRM projects should be supported to achieve this goal? My time-based cost justification approach will help you answer both these questions rationally and in a manner consistent with your financial goals. After explaining this approach, I will also show you why conventional cost-justification approaches would fall short.

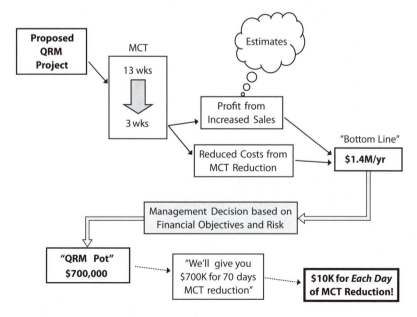

FIGURE 5.1
Time-based project justification approach.

The time-based approach is illustrated in Figure 5.1. With an eye on the goal of a 3-week MCT, you conduct brainstorming sessions with cross-functional teams of employees. As outcomes of these sessions you are looking for two numbers.

The first number is the increased profit from new sales generated as a result of your quick response to customers. Note that what you need is not the increase in sales, but the increase in profit based on current costs of production. Presumably you would start with estimating the amount that sales would go up for the various products involved and then use this to calculate the profit number needed. Suppose the estimate comes to $800,000 per year. (For simplicity I will assume the annual profit increase will remain at this level for a few years, but the calculation in this section can be easily adjusted for multiple years using standard time value of money methods used by financial people.)

The second number you get from these brainstorming sessions is the reduction in costs that will result due to the significantly shorter MCT. You can get to this number in two ways. One is for the teams to identify specific items and put dollar numbers on them—remember to look for not only shop floor impact but also all overheads and system-wide effects as illustrated by the list in Chapter 1. The second way is to use the Power of Six Rule just described. Since it might be difficult to estimate some of the overhead reductions such as less time spent by people in expediting activities, the Power of Six Rule takes care of this by aggregating all these cost reductions into one number. Whichever method you use, you then need to convert the number into an annual amount to get the estimated cost reduction in dollars per year. Let's say the result is $600,000 per year.

Now you add these two numbers (increased profits and reduced costs) to get the figure of $1.4 million per year. This is the net contribution to your bottom line that you can expect from the QRM project. The next step uses traditional financial planning methods. Based on its financial objectives as well as its approach to risk assessment, your executive management must decide how much it is willing to invest in order to get a potential return of $1.4 million per year. This step is no different from what executives already do for proposed projects in their business. Typically companies use criteria such as payback period, net present value (NPV), return on investment (ROI), or internal rate of return (IRR)—sometimes these criteria are also called hurdle rates. For simplicity let's assume for our example that your executives use the payback period approach, and they have different payback period requirements for projects based on the amount of money requested and the perceived risk of the project. In this case they decide to apply a six-month payback period for this project. While this might appear to be a very short period, they have some reasoning behind it. The executives perceive this project to be fairly risky since it is their first QRM project and they are also not quite as confident about magnitude of the cost reductions due to short lead times. Using a short payback period is equivalent to allocating less money to the project, so they are in effect risking less on this project.

A 6-month payback period means that the project should pay off the allocated money in half a year. Since the project is expected to add $1.4 million to the bottom line every year, in half a year the project will pay back $700,000. Hence management decides to allocate $700,000 to the QRM project. However, note that at this stage the money is earmarked, but not actually available to spend. This leads us to the next step, which gets interesting and truly illustrates the use of time-based decision making: management's decision to allocate $700,000 for this QRM project now allows us to put a value on MCT reduction.

The project expects to reduce MCT by 10 weeks, or 70 calendar days. Essentially, your management is saying that it will give you $700,000 for 70 days of MCT reduction. A simple division shows that this means you are being given $10,000 for each day of MCT reduction. This is an important insight. The analysis has helped put a dollar value on each day of MCT reduction. You have connected time back to money! Now you can take advantage of this connection and use it both to set goals for your QRM project teams as well as to fund specific projects. In essence, you will create the equivalent of a hurdle rate but it will be based on time reduction, not financial returns.

Next you initiate some QRM project planning in various areas as needed. Let's say in this case there are opportunities for MCT reduction in the supply chain, in office operations, and in several areas of the shop floor, and so you form planning teams for each of these areas. (In the "Embarking on Your QRM Journey" section, I gave you a detailed road map for how these teams are formed and how they operate.) Each team is charged with the task of using the QRM methodology and principles to come up with recommendations for how they could reduce MCT in their area. Specifically, they must produce a plan that estimates how many days of MCT they can eliminate, and how much money would need to be invested to make their plan operational. The teams are also given a target: For each $10,000 of investment they would need, they should aim to reduce MCT by at least 1 day.

TABLE 5.1

Initial Set of QRM Project Proposals

Project	Requested Investment	MCT Reduction (Target)	MCT Reduction (Estimated)	Comments
Q-ROC for Order Proc.	$30,000	3 days	8 days	Exceeds target
Fabrication Cell	$200,000	20 days	15 days	Needs more brainstorming
Assembly Cell	$90,000	9 days	11 days	Exceeds target
Supply Chain	$150,000	15 days	22 days	Exceeds target

The initial plans presented by four teams are as shown in Table 5.1. The first column shows the area of each project, and the second column shows how much money the team is requesting for that project. Now you apply the MCT value criterion you got from management. Essentially, management said, "For each $10,000 that we give you, you need to reduce MCT by at least 1 day." So let's look at the first team's proposal. They want $30,000. That means they need to reduce MCT by at least 3 days as shown in the third column with the heading "MCT Reduction (Target)." In fact, they estimate that their project will reduce MCT by 8 days (fourth column), so they have essentially exceeded their target as noted in the last column. Thus this project gets funded, and the team proceeds with additional analysis and implementation (again, see the "Embarking on Your QRM Journey" section for details on this).

Your second team wants $200,000 to set up a QRM Cell for some fabrication operations. They should reduce MCT by 20 days to satisfy management's criterion, but currently their proposal cuts only 15 days out of the MCT value. Your feedback to this team is that they need to brainstorm some more and come back with a stronger proposal that reduces MCT by more days. Proceeding with this line of reasoning we see that the next two projects—one for an assembly cell and one working on supply chain issues—both exceed their targets, so they also get funded and can begin their QRM efforts.

After another month of brainstorming and rethinking its options, your second team comes back with a revised proposal. For an investment of $220,000 in a Fabrication Cell, the team estimates it can reduce MCT by 19 days. This still does not meet the criterion. They need to cut MCT by 22 days. But it turns out that the fabrication processes for this product line are complex and time consuming, and it seems difficult to find alternatives

TABLE 5.2

Final Set of QRM Project Proposals

Project	Requested Investment	MCT Reduction (Target)	MCT Reduction (Estimated)	Comments
Q-ROC for Order Proc.	$30,000	3 days	8 days	Exceeds target
Fabrication Cell	$220,000	22 days	19 days	Still short
Assembly Cell	$90,000	9 days	11 days	Exceeds target
Supply Chain	$150,000	15 days	22 days	Exceeds target
Other Projects	$180,000	18 days	19 days	Exceed target
Total	**$670,000**	**67 days**	**79 days**	**Exceeds project goal**

with a shorter MCT. So does this mean the overall QRM project is stalled and you won't ever achieve your final target of 3 weeks' MCT?

Don't worry, all is not lost! In the meantime, a few other projects have been proposed and funded. By this time you have the collection of projects shown in Table 5.2. The first four rows list the same four projects discussed; the numbers for the Fabrication Cell have been updated to their new proposal. The other projects that have been funded in the meantime are summarized in the fifth row: they require $180,000 and should be able to reduce MCT by 19 days. The bottom row in the table sums up the whole basket of projects that have been proposed thus far. Remember that your management was willing to invest $700,000 in order to get an MCT reduction of 70 days. This set of projects requires an investment of only $670,000 and yet it offers an MCT reduction of 79 days. Clearly, your management's criterion has been met—indeed exceeded—and so you can in fact fund the Fabrication Cell project and let that team proceed with implementation as well. At this point you have successfully justified and started implementing a set of projects that should achieve your MCT reduction goal.

So what's unique about this approach to project justification? Figure 5.2 helps to drive home the distinction between this and conventional approaches. In the traditional cost justification approach, your corporate strategy and financial goals lead you to a specific hurdle rate or payback period. Individual projects then have to show sufficient monetary payback to exceed this financial hurdle rate. The problem with this is that often an individual project, by itself, can't achieve any financial goals at all. Let's consider the Assembly Cell project using traditional methods. The current MCT is 13 weeks. If a team proposes this project, it will expect to reduce the MCT by 11 days or about 1.5 weeks. An MCT reduction of this small

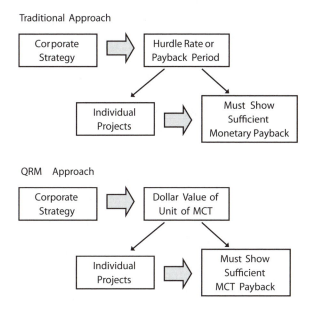

FIGURE 5.2
Comparison of traditional versus QRM approaches to project justification.

amount will neither be significant enough to impact sales and market share, nor substantial enough to reduce total costs. Hence it will be very hard for the team to come up with enough financial savings to justify the $90,000 that it needs.

The time-based cost justification approach also uses your corporate financial goals, but it does so in order to arrive at a value for each day of MCT reduction. Now, individual projects need to show a sufficient MCT reduction in order to be funded. The financial payback criterion has been replaced by an MCT payback criterion. Thus the 11-day MCT reduction offered by the Assembly Cell project allows it to get the $90,000 that it requested. Since the big monetary payback will be seen only once enough projects are in place, it is important for management to keep seeding projects until eventually the results are seen. This is an instance where the whole is greater than the sum of its parts! Each project on its own would produce only marginal financial results at best. But string them together one by one, and when they finally add up to your target, the financial results start to pour in. It is management's job to perceive this strategy and to orchestrate it.

My time-based cost justification approach is not as radical as it may seem at first impression. Note that at the corporate strategy level, this approach is entirely consistent with traditional financial thinking: management sets financial criteria based on strategic goals and its risk tolerance. Hence at this level, financial experts cannot argue against the approach. It is the way that the approach then helps to encourage and seed projects that sets the time-based approach apart, and also makes it a powerful tool to support the implementation of QRM in your company.

USE ACCOUNTING STRATEGIES TO SUPPORT QRM

I have given you many examples of how cost-based decisions lead you in the wrong direction as far as reducing MCT. In Chapter 1, I also showed you how standard cost calculations often predict that QRM will result in higher product costs, whereas in practice the reality of implementing QRM is the opposite: costs go down. If accounting systems assigned overhead accurately to each item based on the actual support and indirect costs incurred for that item, then there would be no problem—as you implemented QRM, direct-labor costs would go up slightly and overhead costs for that item would go down substantially, resulting in an overall cost decrease. The problem in most accounting systems is that overhead costs are simply collected into a plant-wide pool and the overhead cost assigned to the item is an artificial amount, often a percentage of direct labor—so the cost goes up as direct labor goes up, even though overhead for this particular item might be going down as a result of the QRM project. All accounting systems that use allocated overhead or overhead rates have this distortion. Does this mean that your accounting system will always be at odds with QRM? It doesn't have to be that way. A few simple changes to your accounting system can reduce the impact of this distortion and can go a long way toward making your accounting system support your QRM strategy. These changes are completely consistent with GAAP (generally accepted accounting principles) so there is no legal reason not to adopt them; the biggest issue will be the mind-set of your executive management.

The first step to adapting your accounting system should therefore be to get executive management and accounting on board. In particular, instead of constantly having to battle the accountants, expose your top accounting and finance executives to basic education in QRM. Let them review various examples—such as those in this book—where accounting systems impede QRM implementation. This will assist them in understanding the issues and obstacles. Then have them partner with you on designing the changes that your company needs to implement. This will do two things: First, it will ensure that your new methods have the support of top management; and second you can review the ideas in the following sections, and then select the ones most suited to your situation and adapt them for your own use.

With this in mind, here are a number of accounting strategies that will be supportive of your QRM implementation. (*Note:* Some of these strategies were presented by Paul Allen, director of finance at Cardinal Health, Madison, Wisconsin, during conferences held at the Center for Quick Response Manufacturing. Paul has many years of experience in supporting QRM implementation at both Datex-Ohmeda, Madison, Wisconsin, now part of GE Medical Systems, and Cardinal Health.) You can use any one of them that appeals to your executives or even several of them in combination, since the approaches reinforce each other. Hopefully this list will stimulate the generation of additional ideas by your accounting folks and you will end up with a system that works best for your company and its products.

Use Lower Overhead Rates for Cells

A major obstacle to implementing cells and other QRM strategies such as smaller batch sizes is that the direct-labor component appears to increase. This is then magnified by overhead allocations (often 200% or more of the labor cost), so it appears that parts cost much more to be made using QRM methods. In practice, we know that many of the overhead costs go down. Over time, with productivity improvements, the labor cost goes down too, but even without that, as shown in Figure 1.7 in Chapter 1, the overhead reductions usually far exceed the labor cost increases. Unfortunately the accounting system does not predict this. The solution is to decide on different (usually lower) overhead allocation rates for each cell rather than having one plant-wide rate. Depending on the amount of effort you want to invest in this, there are two ways to implement this.

The first is by using *strategic overhead allocation*. Among the suggestions listed here, this is probably the simplest to implement, but it might require the most courage from top management. The idea is for management to obtain a rough estimate of the overhead costs that will be reduced for the FTMS products (remember to include support items that are no longer even needed by the QRM Cells), and use this estimate to decide on a lower overhead allocation rate for the QRM Cells. Initially, this will most likely lead to underabsorption of overhead costs. Normally this would result in "unfavorable variances" and reprimands to factory managers, but management should anticipate this and create a strategic overhead pool where it collects these unabsorbed amounts. Management should give itself a target of how much it expects this pool to fill up and not be concerned prior to this point. Over time, as more and more results are obtained from QRM projects, and also more products are shipped without adding personnel on the shop floor or in the office, the organizational overhead per product will decrease and now management will see overabsorption of overhead. This extra absorption is used to drain the strategic overhead pool until it is empty. Thus management will be content that it has recovered all the costs that appeared to have been overspent. By this time, enough operational data should be available to recalculate the overhead allocation. QRM should also have proven itself clearly by this stage, so that this method is no longer needed.

Note that this approach does not violate GAAP because accounting systems have a way to deal with under- or overabsorption, which already happens to some extent every period. Adjustments are made in the income statement and other reports for this. So the strategic overhead allocation method is primarily a management device and does not change the underlying accounting methods. However, what these accounting adjustments mean is that initially, during the underabsorption period, when the accounting adjustments are made for this, it will appear that you are losing money on some product lines, or even on your entire operation. This is why I said this approach is simple but it needs courage! Management needs to recognize that the business may not be losing any money at all; it's just that the accounting predictions think it is; or if the business is losing some money, that money will be recovered as the QRM strategy takes effect more broadly. Management needs to have the courage to stay the course for these results to occur.

There is another significant advantage to using this approach. Applying the lower overhead value to cost out the products being made in the QRM way allows you to price them more competitively. This results in increased market share, which requires more production, and this in turn leads to even lower costs. Hence the strategic overhead allocation leads to a growing cycle of benefits.

I will now explain the second, more detailed way to apply overhead based on cells, and this is by *determining an allocation rate* for each cell by explicitly assigning overhead to that cell. The idea here is to assign directly to each cell as many support and indirect costs as can be identified with that cell. For instance, in a shop floor cell, if you can account for tooling and supplies used only by the cell, then those costs become part of the overhead assigned to the cell. Conversely, if a cell no longer uses a particular support function (such as expediting) that is part of the overall overhead, or uses much less of it, then that should be excluded from (or much reduced in) the assignment to the cell. All of these efforts will help assign costs where they belong and minimize distortions. Following this, you still have to allocate what remains of the company-wide overhead to cells. For this, keep the approach simple. For example, factory support staff can be allocated to cells based on short interviews and surveys to determine where they are used, and factory fixed costs can be allocated based on floor space or total hours of production in each cell. Finally, you need to allocate the resulting overhead pool assigned to the cell down to individual products going through the cell—again you should keep this simple for two reasons. One is that the FTMS derivation has already ensured that products going through the cell share similar characteristics. The other is that since the overhead rate for the cell will generally be much lower after the preceding calculations, there is less misallocation to worry about. So now you can even allocate overhead within the cells based on labor hours because much of the distortion I have previously discussed will have been removed through these procedures.

Assign Overhead Using More than Just Direct Labor

When you consider that direct labor accounts for only around 10% of your cost of goods sold, it seems strange that many companies still use mainly labor to allocate overheads. Think of this: in addition to the direct-labor time, a typical job requires time from people in sales, order entry, engineering, materials planning, scheduling, purchasing, and shipping, just to name some of the key ones. Then why do we allocate costs based only on labor time? Obviously this will lead to misallocations of overhead for different types of jobs. There is a simple fix that you can make. It takes more work than the previous idea, but it can still be kept from getting out of hand. The idea is to quantify some key processes that are required for jobs and to cost those out directly. (This may sound the same as activity-based costing, but my approach is much simpler and requires much less time and data.)

I'll illustrate the approach with an example. For a given product line, a rough analysis shows that it takes on average 20 minutes of Inside Sales' time, 10 minutes of Order Entry's time, 30 minutes of Engineering's time, 40 minutes of Purchasing's time (based on the various components needed and how often they are ordered), and so on. (*Note:* All these times I have stated are touch times, when someone is actually working on the job.) For each of these processes, get your accountants to calculate "local" hourly rates for the times. By this I mean the costs that are incurred in that area including local overhead costs, but not company-wide overhead. For instance, in addition to the salary and benefits of the order entry operators, if that area uses computers and has a supervisor, the depreciation for the computers and the salary of the supervisor should be included in the rate calculation. On the shop floor you can calculate an hourly rate for labor and separately an hourly rate for each machine (to do a better job of costing out jobs that use more expensive machines). For a given job, you now use all these hourly rates to calculate the direct cost of all the processes for this job. Finally, you allocate a share of the remaining corporate overhead to the job as I will explain soon.

While more detailed than just using labor to allocate overhead, this approach has a significant advantage. It takes all these direct costs out of the overhead pool and assigns them to the jobs that use them; thus it reduces the amount of the remaining overhead pool that gets allocated, and hence reduces the distortion due to misallocation. In other words, since a lot more costs are being accounted for directly, and a lot less are being allocated, you can allocate the remaining corporate overhead using simple rules to spread it over each of these areas. Even if many of your estimates for all these costs are rough, you will still do a much better job than the current system that uses only labor to allocate all costs.

In addition to doing a better job of assigning costs in general, this approach supports QRM because the additional labor time required for QRM-related improvements is less amplified or even canceled out through reduction of other costs. Figure 5.3 illustrates this point. In the upper part of the figure, you see labor-based cost allocation. The labor is for the setup and run time of a job, and this gets amplified with the overhead burden to produce the long bar at the top. Now if you cut the batch size of this product in half, for the same final run quantity you now have to do two setups. The labor for this additional setup also gets amplified by the burden so the total cost of the same run quantity goes up substantially. It becomes difficult to argue that QRM improvements will cancel out this large additional cost.

In the lower part of the figure, you see overhead allocation based on a number of processes, not just direct labor. Now, since many more costs are directly accounted for, the magnification due to overhead allocation

Predicted Impact of Smaller Batches When You Use Direct Labor-based Overhead Allocation

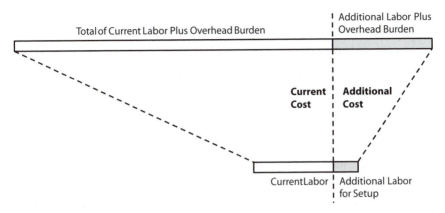

Predicted Impact of Smaller Batches When You Identify Additional Direct Costs and Then Apply Overhead

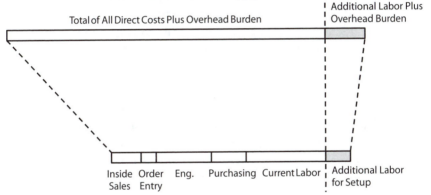

FIGURE 5.3
Using other direct costs (in addition to labor) reduces the predicted negative impact of smaller batches.

is much less. When you cut the batch size, the additional labor for setup increases the cost by only a small amount. It is much easier now to get management to buy in to the smaller batch size as you can probably point to several other improvements through QRM that will reduce costs by more than this amount.

I'd like to add a point here that is not related to cost but to performance measurement in general. Most companies still measure direct-labor efficiency; but as I mentioned earlier, if direct labor is only 10% of your cost, this measure is misguided. Since many other people are involved in order fulfillment as shown in the preceding example, a better measure would be to look at the ratio of total shipments to the total headcount at the site—this would include both shop floor and office personnel and do a better job of indicating the productivity of your organization as a whole. As just one example, if cell teams took on roles that eliminated quite a few office tasks, the traditional labor efficiency measure would suffer, but with the total site headcount approach there might be no negative impact, or better still, a positive impact on the measure.

Apply Overhead at the Time of Shipment

This is a novel idea but truly supports QRM for several reasons. In companies where factory managers are under pressure to meet their targets of overhead absorption, there is a tendency to make things just to meet this absorption target in each period. Otherwise you get what is called an unfavorable variance in the accounting report, and this makes the factory manager look "inefficient." So when managers feel they are not going to make the target, they pull jobs ahead in the schedule or make items to stock in larger quantities than required, just to get the overhead absorption on the greater production hours. Clearly these efforts add to your MCT and go against everything I've discussed in this book.

Now what if your accounting system wouldn't allow you to count the overhead absorption on an item until after that item had been shipped—what would this do to your operations? First, it would prevent unneeded overproduction—your factory manager wouldn't get any "points" if the items made were not being shipped during the period. More interesting is a second effect: it would encourage reduction of MCT. Why? Because as soon as you start working on a job, you use material, labor, and other direct costs that show up in the accounting report and add to your expenses for that period. But if the job does not ship, you don't get the "points" for overhead absorption. This means that you should start jobs as close as possible to their ship dates and not have anything sitting around—in other words, this overhead allocation scheme gives you an incentive to reduce your MCT.

Apply Overhead Based on MCT or Other Lead Time Measure

Since QRM advocates that a substantial amount of your overhead costs are driven by MCT, an approach that would totally support QRM would be to allocate overhead based on MCT for each job, FTMS, or product line. If MCT is hard to calculate in your system (because, say, specific parts cannot be tracked through stocking points), a simpler alternative would be to allocate overhead to each work order based on the time that work order is open. Or you can use any other similar measure that works in your situation, as long as it has a reasonable connection to MCT.

Reassign Some of the Overhead Costs Specifically to Large Batches

In this book I have given you many examples of increased overhead costs due to large batches and long lead times. Unfortunately, most of those costs disappear into a large overhead pool and are not correctly assigned. You can create a few simple rules to fix this. For example, think of all the costs related to finished goods, such as warehouse space, material handling, interest, cycle counting, spoilage, obsolescence, and others. Now consider why you carry finished goods at all. The two most common reasons are that your lead time is too long to make to order; or due to standard cost calculations, you decide to build more than you need to ship. Suppose for a given product the average customer order is for 100 pieces, but due to standard cost considerations in the past you have a policy to make 500 pieces at a time. Then you are making 400 parts more that the customer requires at a given time. This excess quantity results in finished goods. So the idea is to pull the costs related to finished goods out of your overhead pool and assign them to parts built in excess quantities. Using historical data you can get a value for the total excess quantities built over a year, as well as the total costs of carrying finished goods converted to an annual cost. You can use these numbers to come up with a simple rule to allocate the cost of finished goods to excess quantities. Now if you want to run a batch size of 500 when the customer needs only 100, the additional 400 pieces will get allocated this additional burden. You have created an incentive to run smaller batches.

Remembering that large batches result in long MCT with many dysfunctional effects such as expediting, repeated forecasting and scheduling, and others discussed in this book, you could also try to get rough estimates for these effects and pull some of those costs out of overhead and burden the batch size with them. This will create an even greater incentive to run smaller batches. As your smaller batches result in shorter Flow Times and lower MCT, you will get lower overhead costs and hence it will be easier to justify even smaller batches and thus move closer and closer to a make-to-order operation. Note that this whole approach is consistent with GAAP because the overhead is still being allocated to products; it's just being allocated differently.

Combine Approaches for Better Results

As a reminder to my earlier statement, two or more of these methods can be combined with even more powerful effect. For instance, if you combine the last four approaches of quantifying as many direct costs as possible at the cell level, applying overhead only when items ship, using MCT to allocate the overhead, and burdening excess quantities, you would achieve several goals: more accurately assigned cost, incentives for MCT reduction, and incentives for batch size reduction.

RECOGNIZE THAT YOUR EXISTING IMPROVEMENT STRATEGIES STRENGTHEN YOUR QRM PROGRAM

Manufacturing strategy today abounds with acronyms and techniques such as JIT (just-in-time), Kaizen, SMED (single-minute exchange of dies), Lean, Six Sigma, and many others. If you are already using some of these techniques in your organization, you might wonder whether embarking on the QRM journey means that you have to abandon these methods and replace them with QRM techniques. That is not the case at all. Quite to the contrary, QRM can help support and focus these methods so that they provide more productive results. This is a huge benefit to rolling out your QRM strategy. Employees often complain about the "flavor of the month" approach by management, where new programs and buzzwords are brought in frequently and previous ones are forgotten. With QRM you don't have to reverse gears at all. Rather, the message to your employees can be a positive one: "With QRM, we are building on all the tools we have used thus far, and moreover, QRM will take us to newer heights in our ability to apply these tools for strategic advantage." I will now explain why this is the case.

As you proceed to tackle a QRM project using the road map I provided and start to apply the various QRM tools that you have learned—FTMS, QRM Cells, Q-ROCs, batch size reduction, and others—you will encounter some challenges. At this point you might recognize that one of these other manufacturing strategies has just the tools needed to overcome one of these challenges. Let me give you a few concrete examples:

- You have implemented a QRM Cell and the team has started reducing batch sizes for the parts going through the cell. As it does so, it realizes that a CNC mill is becoming a bottleneck and a lot of its capacity is going into changeover times. This is a perfect opportunity to bring in your SMED expert to help the team since SMED provides many specific techniques to reduce changeover times. Thus an effective SMED project in this cell will support the overall QRM implementation.

- In the early stages of its operation, a Q-ROC team responsible for order processing for a line of products notices that many small errors are creeping into the orders they release to the shop floor. This is an opportunity for a Six Sigma project focused on finding the root causes of these problems so that they can be fixed. If you already have Six Sigma training and expertise in your organization, the Q-ROC can take advantage of that expertise to conduct a Six Sigma project and improve its operation. Again, we see how the QRM approach provides the focus for a Six Sigma project, which, in turn, strengthens the results of the QRM implementation.

- If you have already conducted some Lean training and there are people who know how to perform Value Stream Mapping (VSM), then it will be easy to apply that knowledge to create MCT maps for QRM projects. MCT maps require less detail and present the data with an emphasis on the time line, but a lot of the basic data to be gathered is similar to that in VSM. Here too we have an example of how the tools that you already have invested in from another approach can be used to support your QRM efforts. Moreover, as pointed out in Chapter 1, QRM does not undermine your Lean efforts, but rather it takes your Lean strategy to the next level with an ability to tackle more difficult customers and market opportunities.

Looking at these examples, perhaps you are asking why it couldn't be the other way around. For instance, why not adopt Kaizen as the main strategy and then have QRM and other strategies support your Kaizen efforts? The answer is clear from my arguments in Chapter 1. Time is a lot more money than most people realize, and if you can take advantage of this and reduce time (MCT) in your organization, you can be very successful. QRM is the only comprehensive, enterprise-wide strategy that has the single-minded focus as well as the set of tools to help you reduce time. In contrast, Kaizen is a generic continuous improvement approach—this makes it powerful in that it can be applied to target any improvement goal, but at the same time it does not offer tools that are specifically geared toward lead time reduction. Another comment made to me by many managers involved in QRM projects is that while Kaizen projects can be done quickly, they tend to be "local" in their scope and hence limited in their impact, while QRM through its focus on MCT always forces you to take a "global" view of the situation, with greater scope for significant impact on your operations.

Similar comments apply to Six Sigma—a generic quality improvement strategy, but again without tools that are specifically geared toward lead time reduction. As a pointed illustration of this assertion, ask yourself where in Kaizen or Six Sigma literature have you seen discussions on the implication of capacity on lead time, such as the graphs that I showed you in Chapter 3? They are simply not part of those techniques.

If you are convinced about the power of time and want to capitalize on it, then QRM has to be your driving strategy. However, all the past organizational effort you have put into developing expertise in other strategies will not be wasted at all. QRM will build on all that expertise and sharpen its application in support of your MCT reduction efforts.

USE QRM AS A POSITIVE, UNIFYING PERSPECTIVE FOR YOUR ENTIRE BUSINESS

At any point in time, if you examine the set of ongoing improvement activities at an organization such as yours, you will find a number of approaches being used in different areas of the organization, with most of them having diverse goals. You will probably also find multiple approaches with different aims within the same area of the organization! This typically leads to conflicting priorities or even opposing efforts. There is also competition for people's beliefs as employees are trained in all these apparent dogmas—perhaps even resulting in employee apathy as they don't buy in to any approach—"Just wait a while and we'll be asked to do something else anyway!" is a common thought.

In contrast, the QRM message is simple to understand, singular in its focus, and applies to every aspect of the enterprise, and so everyone in the organization can be aligned behind one single goal—reduce MCT. There is another advantage in terms of how the message is perceived; when you tell employees that they must be "more efficient" or that you need to become "more lean," what they hear is that you want them to work harder for less pay, or that you need to eliminate some "fat" in the enterprise and what if they are part of this fat? So those messages may not go over well. On the other hand, if you explain to your employees that your company needs to be more responsive to customers in order to stay competitive, and then ask them what they can do to help with this goal, you will find that they will step up to the challenge. As Terry Nelson, former vice president of continuous improvement at Rockwell Automation in Milwaukee, Wisconsin, once said to me (explaining why he was convinced about the potency of QRM), "Focus on responsiveness is a positive, unifying perspective for the entire business."

I have now shown you the full competitive power of QRM: how responsiveness helps you gain market share; how reduction of MCT lowers your costs and improves quality; how the QRM organization energizes your employees; and many other benefits. It is now time for you to launch your enterprise on the QRM journey and leap ahead of your competition to become the leader in your industry.

Index

About the Author

Rajan Suri is Emeritus Professor of Industrial Engineering at the University of Wisconsin–Madison. He received his bachelor's degree from Cambridge University (England) in 1974, and his M.S. and Ph.D. from Harvard University in 1978.

Dr. Suri founded and served as director of the Center for Quick Response Manufacturing (QRM) from 1993 to 2008, and he continues to serve the Center in an advisory role. The Center is a consortium of companies working with the university on understanding and implementing QRM strategies—over 200 companies have worked with and supported the activities of the Center (see www.qrmcenter.org). Dr. Suri is internationally regarded as an expert on the analysis of manufacturing systems and is author of the book *Quick Response Manufacturing: A Companywide Approach to Reducing Lead Times* (540 pages, Productivity Press, 1998). He is also author of over 100 technical publications, has chaired several international conferences on manufacturing systems, and has served on the editorial boards of leading scholarly journals in the field of manufacturing.

Professor Suri also served as director of the Manufacturing Systems Engineering Program at the University of Wisconsin–Madison for 15 years. This is an interdisciplinary, practice-oriented M.S. degree program housed within the College of Engineering, with strong ties to the School of Business. Graduates of the program are highly qualified to assist manufacturing firms in implementing practices that will make them more competitive.

Dr. Suri combines his academic credentials with considerable practical experience. He has consulted for leading firms including 3M, Alcoa, AT&T, Danfoss, Ford, Hewlett-Packard, Hitachi, IBM, Ingersoll, John Deere, National Oilwell Varco, P&H Mining Equipment, Pratt & Whitney, Rockwell Automation, Siemens, and TREK Bicycle. Consulting assignments in Europe and the Far East, along with projects for the World Bank, have given him a substantial international perspective on manufacturing competitiveness.

In 1981, Dr. Suri received the Eckman Award from the American Automatic Control Council for outstanding contributions in his field. He was a member of the team that received the 1988 LEAD Award from the Society of Manufacturing Engineers. He is coauthor of a paper that won the 1990 Outstanding Simulation Publication Award from the Institute of

Management Sciences. In 1994, he was co-recipient of the IEEE Control Systems Technology Award. In 1999, Dr. Suri was made a Fellow of the Society of Manufacturing Engineers (SME), and in 2006, he received SME's Albert M. Sargent Progress Award for the creation and implementation of the Quick Response Manufacturing philosophy.